The Captive Mind

The Captive Mind

JADA EDWARDS

The Captive Mind, by Jada Edwards

First Printing, 2016.

ISBN-10: 0-578-18680-1
ISBN-13: 978-0-578-18680-1

Printed in the U.S.A.

Dedication

For you Conway,
my love and my partner.
You inspire me. You believe in me.
I am better because of you.

For you Granny,
your faith and character have shaped me in ways
I'll never understand.
You were my first mentor.
Your value is far above rubies.

For you Dad and Mom,
your love, guidance and support have given me the freedom to fly.
You set the example for everything.
Thank you.

PRAISE FOR *THE CAPTIVE MIND*

The Captive Mind is the perfect roadmap for transformation that provides a Biblical strategy to change everyday living into an extraordinary experience. With her natural gift of clear and authentic communication, Jada will guide you through the process of examining yourself and unlocking God's armory of resources. You are now invited to embark on a journey that moves you from simply conforming to circumstances to intentionally responding through God's Word. Prepare to be changed forever.

Dr. Conway Edwards
Lead Pastor, One Community Church, Plano, Texas

If there was ever a faithful student, humble servant and articulate minister of God's Word, it is Jada Edwards. The depth of insight that she gleans from Scripture and then communicates is astounding. Gleaning from her wisdom has been one of the great inspirations for my own personal spiritual formation as well as my public ministry. The book you are holding in your hands is a game changer. The truths on each page will sink into the depths of your soul and unroot the strongholds that threaten your journey toward abundance and destiny. If you'll commit to not only reading this work but molding your thought lifeaccording to its lessons, the entire trajectory of your life - and even the lives of the people you love the most - will be set on a course toward joy and victory.

Priscilla Shirer

Author of *The Armor of God* and *The Prince Warriors*

Jada has the unique ability to break important, life-changing spiritual principles into practical, bite-sized chunks with uncommon wit, humor, and power that pierces the heart while moving the listener to take action with their feet. She is a dynamic teacher and speaker with a gift to articulate the truth of God's Word with clarity and precision and her Bible Study will prove to be no different. I am excited about Jada's gift to communicate spiritual truths and the crucial nature of this topic. The Captive Mind is a study that will be a blessing to many as they learn more about the power of God at work in their thoughts and therefore in their everyday lives.

Chrystal Hurst

Author of *Kingdom Woman*

I am incredibly thankful for the day I was introduced to Jada Edwards. There was an instant connection and it has been a tremendous joy to watch her in ministry. Her sincere heart, bubbly personality, and powerful teaching are so enjoyable. Jada has a gift of teaching that seems to always leave you wanting more. Captive Heart is a true reflection of her ability to speak truth to important matters in all of our lives. Sometimes life can catch us off guard and we find ourselves searching for words. Captive Mind is like talking to your best friend and giving you the advice, wisdom, and encouragement you need to live boldly for Christ. You will be deeply enriched by this work.

Stephanie Carter,

Women's Ministry Leader, Concord Church, Dallas, Texas

Contents

Foreword by Dr. Tony Evans

One of the great rewards of ministry is to see children you have spiritually fathered in the faith launch out and be used by God to serve Him and His people in ministry. This is why I was honored when my spiritual daughter, Jada, asked me to write the foreword for her first book, *The Captive Mind.* To see her express herself so fluently and biblically on the power and importance of being spiritually minded if we are going to experience victory in our spiritual walk is a joy for me and a message we all need to hear.

As every serious Christian knows, "as a man thinketh so is he." Until our minds are consistently under the control of the Holy Spirit, we become easy bait for the evil one to deceive us and wreak havoc in our lives. Unless we win the battle for the mind, we can never hope to be victorious in all the other battles we face. Without a transformed mind it is impossible to have a transformed life.

Jada gives us a challenging yet realistic look at the critical roll our thinking plays in our decisions and how these decisions can render us victorious or victors in the cosmic battle for our souls. In this work Jada not only discusses the nature of the battle, but more importantly the road to victory as we learn to develop a Christ-captivated mind. You will be encouraged and challenged to understand and utilize the spiritual resources at your disposal to thwart the enemy's attacks against you as you learn to change your thinking.

It is my prayer that God will use this book to strengthen the struggling believers and confirm to those who are standing strong that nothing can defeat the child of God whose mind has been taken captive by Christ.

Dr. Tony Evans
Senior Pastor, Oak Cliff Bible Fellowship
President, The Urban Alternative

Introduction

An invisible, intangible thought has the power to change everything in the most visible and tangible of ways.

I couldn't believe what I was hearing.

Not too long ago, I received a phone call with news that rocked me to my core. It was a tragedy unlike anything I'd ever experienced. Two good friends of mine, a husband and wife who had been a part of our ministry for many years, lost their lives in a homicide-suicide shooting.

They had endured many highs and lows in their short marriage and to say their relationship was an emotional roller coaster would be putting it mildly. But to me and my husband, these issues are common among married couples. We counseled them and invited them into a small community of other married couples in hopes their marriage would be strengthened. We thought we did all the right things.

Prayer. Counseling. Scripture. Small groups. Ministry service.

But nothing was enough. Nothing we did kept these two hurting people from this very tragic end. Very few things make you reevaluate your beliefs like sudden and devastating death.

One night, as I was mourning this loss, something woke me up. Well not just something, *Someone.* I was roused from my sleep with one phrase, "Take every thought captive." I began mentally wrestling with the dark reality that a person who knows the love of the Lord can get to such a dark place that the best option seems to be taking the life of a spouse, and then taking his or her own life.

Not too long after that incident, I had a couple of friends share their struggles of depression and anxiety with me. They battled dark and suicidal thoughts. They weren't simply having hard days or going through a tough season. My friends were battling moment to moment to get through an average day. I couldn't comprehend that I had friends who spent their energy with little hope of surviving rather than thriving in the hope we have in Christ. They were so far from the abundance and joy that should mark the life of a believer that no quick prayer or pat answer would change their courses. Now, I wasn't ignorant. I knew those kinds of emotional/mental situations were out there but I never expected them to land on my doorstep.

In a matter of weeks, I had encountered men and women who were followers of Jesus but living without joy. They were lost. Hopeless. Desperate. They had become slaves to their minds instead of masters of their minds. In the midst of processing this tragedy, I had a moment where printed words and quoted verses instantly became living truth.

We are at war.

The fight is not against flesh and blood. We must take every thought captive. See, every believer is a volunteer warrior. The war begins in the soul but quickly moves to the mind.

When the idea for this book came to me, I wasn't even thinking about Bible study. I was trying to relax. However, in the middle of the night I just woke up with three words running through my mind on repeat. God said to me, "Every thought captive. Every thought captive. Every thought captive."

What does that even mean?

It means intentional effort to know truth and dispel lies. It means uprooting the seeds of sinful thinking before they bear fruit. It means that even if they've taken root, you can demolish them before they take over.

It's time for a new approach. Modifying behavior isn't a long-term solution. We can't sustain different behavior if we don't have different beliefs. So here's my invitation. Do a little investigation with me and see what God has to say about all this. Discover how you can evict old thinking and experience new life.

ONE
A NEW REACTION

"Do not be conformed to this world, but be transformed by the renewal of your mind, that by testing you may discern what is the will of God, what is good and acceptable and perfect."
(Romans 12:2)

In junior high school, I was a very active cross country runner. For many people, running is something you either love or hate. Well, I *loved* to run. I didn't run a lot of races on nice neat tracks. I was usually in some nature preserve or on a trail. The best places for challenging runs provided plenty of opportunities to trip over rocks, dodge snakes, and stumble over tree roots.

On one particular run I saw a rock. The problem was, I saw it just a second too late. I hit the ground and everything was a blur after that. I tried to brace myself, but in my attempt to break my fall, I ended up doing more damage. I had cuts and scratches everywhere. I remember going back to school and my coach saying to me, "Jada, I'm going to tell you what your problem is. You don't know how to fall."

Wait. What? Is there a way to fall?

I answered and said, "I thought the goal was not to fall." He quickly replied with, "No, no, no. That's not a reasonable goal because you're always going to fall. The goal is to know how to fall."

He had to explain it to me, and it took several weeks for me to learn the correct way to fall. This art of adjusting your body is used often in martial arts and it can be applied to running and other sports where you might come in contact with the ground. They're teaching you to mentally slow down the process. It's kind of like seeing it before it actually happens. You don't use your hands and you follow your instincts. You roll your body and tuck, and if your right foot twists, you want to fall to the right; you don't want to try to counter it because it's going to make your fall worse. There is a whole list of things on the good and healthy way to fall.

Who knew?

Being intentional about something can birth new instinct.

The reason it was hard for me to learn the correct way to fall was because my brain had a default wiring when it came to falling. If my body looked like it was about to hit the ground, my brain would send out a signal that said, *Body, engage to break this fall.* My brain was not trying to assess which foot was twisting or which way I needed to tuck and roll. It was being reactive and instinctive. My coach was attempting to counter that instinctive reaction with retraining. His aim was to get me to practice a different response long enough to develop a new reaction. You see, being intentional about something can actually birth new instinct.

When I thought about the subject of *The Captive Mind*, I came to the realization that initially this choice to take thoughts captive is counterintuitive. It requires awareness that our minds have a default, or reactive way to respond to circumstances and to environments that we find ourselves in. As we advance through this book, we'll see how the Bible is going to challenge us to retrain our minds to produce different responses. As we continue to yield to the Holy Spirit, those intentional, counterintuitive responses can ultimately become instinctive reactions.

To truly begin to capture or control our thinking means we are looking beyond mere behavior modification. We don't simply want to act better, we want to *think* better. It's easy to spend energy on improving outcomes and behaviors instead of focusing on our beliefs.

We don't simply want to act better, we want to think better.

I want more than just the absence of anxiety, depression, addiction, and suicidal thoughts. Let's reach for higher goals than ending bad relationships, getting out of debt, losing weight, and raising "good kids." Those are definitely things that should change and I know God can heal and restore. But He also wants us to pursue more than just visible results. He wants us to have a renewed mind. Godly stewardship is greater than getting out of debt. A new mindset on nutrition is better than just losing weight. You may not get speeding tickets or get in car accidents but that doesn't mean you have a safe and defensive mindset about driving. If a new way of thinking is the goal; truth is the path.

When we don't fully understand the truth of God, we fall for whatever is popular. We are vulnerable to choosing popularity over principle. Only God's principles, His Word, His truth can set our minds free from the many lies that hold us hostage. KNOWING TRUTH AND CHOOSING TRUTH IS THE DIFFERENCE BETWEEN AN INFORMED MIND AND A CAPTIVE ONE. Don't expect to just float along ignorant of the war for your mind. Your mind is going to be influenced by something. You must decide if that influence will be truth or lies. We are at war and there is no neutrality in warfare. It's time to engage our minds.

TWO

WE ARE AT WAR

"For though we walk in the flesh,
we are not waging war according to the flesh."
(2 Corinthians 10:3)

Can you recall what you were doing on September 11, 2001? I would venture to say the majority of Americans, and probably a large part of the rest of the world remembers. It was a day that changed many aspects of American life. The events of that day gave birth to a new kind of war - "The War on Terror" - and it quickly became a household phrase. You don't have to agree with how the American government handled that situation. You don't even have to agree with the premise of this ongoing campaign. But one thing is inarguable: on that day, many years ago, the American population became acutely aware that the rules of war had changed. This battle would go beyond what could be seen and take place amongst the shadows. The way we were accustomed to fighting would need to change if we stood a chance of protecting our homeland.

This is the essence of Paul's message in 2 Corinthians 10:3.

Paul starts off by saying something very important; "For though we walk in the flesh..."

Anytime you see "though" or "although" in Scripture, it lets you know the writer is about to present a contrast. Paul begins by stating a simple truth.

We walk in the flesh.

He's talking about physically walking, moving, and functioning. This is basic acknowledgment of our humanity. We're not spiritual beings yet. We're not angels. We don't have super powers. We walk in the flesh. It's the same sentiment he expresses in Galatians 2:20 where he says, "I've been crucified with Christ; and it's no longer I who live, but Christ who lives in me; and the life I now live in the flesh. I live by faith in the Son of God, who loved me and gave Himself up for me."

We do not war according to the flesh.

After stating that simple point, he drops the conflict statement on us. In 2 Corinthians 5:10 he says, "We do not war according to the flesh." Wait. Whoa. What? That's a loaded statement. First, it implies that we are at war. See, in order to explain *how* we do war, we have to establish that we are *at* war. Secondly, we learn that despite our everyday existence being something physical and tangible, that is not the way we engage in war.

You see the phrase "according to"? It means something is subject to a certain set of rules. If you say you're going to live according to the rules of my house, that means you're going to subject yourself to whatever my instructions are in my home. Paul is telling us that while we're physically found in the flesh, we don't subject ourselves to the rules of the flesh when it comes to this war. This may all seem very elementary but don't skip it. Don't rush past this foundation that's being laid. This verse provides an important paradigm shift. When Paul speaks of the flesh he is not only referring to the purely physical nature of our skin and bones but also the moral frailties of our humanity.

In verse 4, he expands on this thought by declaring, "*For the weapons of our warfare are not of the flesh, but have divine power.*" Think about this, I am an American, but when I go to Jamaica, even though I walk as an American, I don't live according to America's rules because I'm in another place. I am still who I am, but the food is different, the laws are different, the currency is different. That's the duality Paul is conveying. Yes, you're in the flesh, but the war is taking place in the spiritual realm. Don't bring strategies of the flesh and think you're going to have success in a spiritual war.

Don't bring the strategies of the flesh and think you're going to have success in a spiritual war.

You must understand that the flesh and the Spirit are at odds with each other. They have different desires and opposing goals. The flesh seeks what feels good today and functions from a self-centered perspective while the Spirit seeks what glorifies God and functions from a perspective of sacrificial love. The idea of spiritual warfare is really where I want to lay some foundation because although this is not a new idea, it's often overlooked or oversimplified. It started when Satan fell from heaven and it has continued throughout the history of mankind. In the Old Testament we have many examples of physical manifestations of spiritual warfare through various wars and battles. God kept sending the Israelites to conquer people groups over and over.

There were often spiritual implications because God's promises were being fulfilled as Israel was conquering territory. In addition to His promises being fulfilled, Satan's kingdom was being diminished because those who they conquered were often evil and pagan people groups.

One particular passage that shows us what spiritual warfare looked like in the Old Testament is found in Exodus, chapter 17. In Exodus 17:8-16, we read:

> 8 Then Amalek came and fought with Israel at Rephidim. 9 So Moses said to Joshua, "Choose for us men, and go out and fight with Amalek. Tomorrow I will stand on the top of the hill with the staff of God in my hand." 10 So Joshua did as Moses told him, and fought with Amalek, while Moses, Aaron, and Hur went up to the top of the hill. 11 Whenever Moses held up his hand, Israel prevailed, and whenever he lowered his hand, Amalek prevailed. 12 But Moses' hands grew weary, so they took a stone and put it under him, and he sat on it, while Aaron and Hur held up his hands, one on one side, and the other on the other side. So his hands were steady until the going down of the sun. 13 And Joshua overwhelmed Amalek and his people with the sword. 14 Then the LORD said to Moses, "Write this as a memorial in a book and recite it in the ears of Joshua, that I will utterly blot out the memory of Amalek from under heaven." 15 And Moses built an altar and called the name of it, The LORD Is My Banner, 16 saying, "A hand upon the throne of the LORD! The LORD will have war with Amalek from generation to generation."

To the casual observer this may look like just another Old Testament battle. Men claim, conquer, blah, blah, blah. But wait. Look closer. There are so many spiritual implications. First of all, the timing of this battle was no coincidence. The Israelites had just crossed the Red Sea. They were on top of the world, so to speak. God had just freed them from Pharaoh, then opened up a body of water so they could walk across on dry land. And to top it off, He brought down manna from heaven when they were wondering how they were going to eat in the wilderness. God was working big-time miracles. Israel, for one of those brief windows in time, was in good standing with God. Everything was going well.

Then came the Amalekites. We read in verse 8: "Then Amalek came and fought against Israel..." Israel didn't do anything to instigate this. The word *Amalekites* means dweller of the valley. The idea that the dweller of the valley came and fought against Israel gives us a glimpse into how significant this battle was because the Israelites were in the middle of a mountaintop experience. Sometimes it's right after God has done something miraculous that a dweller of the valley will come against you. Right after a "spiritual win" God will often remind you that you're in a spiritual war. You don't see where it's coming from or why it's coming. You don't know what caused it. You didn't instigate it. The enemy started the fight, and God allowed it. (Can you hear Job saying, "Been there. Done that."?) He will take you from the mountain top to the valley in the blink of an eye.

Right after a "spiritual win" God will often remind us that we are in a spiritual war.

But don't despise the valley. Good things can happen there. Let the fuel from a fresh victory get you through the valley. When the Amalekites came, the Israelites didn't say, "We can't handle this; this is too much." The Amalekites attacked and Israel prevailed. However, not because of their skill and their war strategy in the flesh. They succeeded because Moses' hands were held up in surrender. Now that is divine power! If that is not a miracle of God, I don't know what is. I have never heard of the elevation of a body part securing victory in battle. The case is clear. These men were made of flesh and bone but they fought according to the Spirit of God.

Moses affirmed this when he built an altar and named it "The LORD is my banner" (Jehovah Nissi). He knew their miraculous victory had only occurred because they fought in the name of Jehovah. Regardless of Moses' military prowess and strategic planning, he knew the victory was spiritual and this same truth applies to us today.

However, understanding this academically and applying it are two different things. Many of us know we should walk according to the Spirit, but we really walk according to the flesh. We walk according to our own logic. It needs to makes sense to us or be comfortable for us and that's a quick way to failure. Trust me. And you don't have to see it for it to be true or acknowledge it for it to be real.

When our son was a baby, like many little ones, he loved playing peek-a-boo. They love this game because around this age they're learning the idea of what is called "object permanence." This concept teaches that *objects continue to exist even when they can't be observed.* My son soon realize that covering his eyes for a moment didn't change my presence.

This same thing is true of spiritual warfare. Just because I cover my eyes and act like I don't see it, does not mean it's going to go away.

But this concept is a comfort regarding God and His love. I may not see Him, but I believe He is there. Ephesians 6 (which we'll dive into later) says, "We don't fight against flesh and blood." Romans 8:38 reads, "*I am sure that neither death nor life, nor angels nor rulers, nor things present nor things to come, nor powers, nor height nor depth, nor anything else in all creation, can separate us from the love of God in Christ Jesus our Lord.*"

Understanding the nature of the battle is the first point of preparation. I can give up my plan of attack and raise my hands in surrender to the Spirit of God. I can start looking beyond what I see with my eyes and search for the subtle spiritual attacks of the enemy. The problems at my job aren't really about the job. The strain in my marriage is really not about my spouse, the house, or the kids. The emotional void in my relationships isn't just because I'm not a people person. My distance from God isn't just about how often I memorize Scripture or attend Bible study.

There are some flaws in our thinking that, if not taken captive by truth, will hold us hostage with lies. They will secretly seep into our souls and bend our beliefs. Then those new beliefs will affect our behavior.

So what does your spiritual battle look like? What might Satan bring your way? Well, the truth is, even though as Christians we are engaged in spiritual warfare, the spiritual battle looks different in each of our lives but it's still the same darkness. Satan is crafty. He is going to acclimate; he is going to customize his attack for you, for your culture, for your family. He wants to win. He doesn't want to be found out so he's going to go undercover.

Satan's attack is going to look very different depending on who you are and depending on your life story. He has observed you from the beginning. You were under his rule before you chose Christ so you're not new to him. That's why God told Cain in Genesis 4:7, "*Sin is crouching at your door.*" He was warning Cain so he would understand the devil was waiting, at the right moment, at the right opportunity, to pounce on him. He is waiting to connect with your flesh so he can counter the truth of God. How might he attack? What will that attack look like? Well, I can share with you a few passages of Scripture that show us how Satan attacks.

The Bible tells us that he is the father of lies and his nature is falsehood. He opposes God's Word. He casts doubt on God's goodness. He destroys the obedience of faith. He hinders the gospel mission. He opposes truth that is reaching and converting people and he will seek to shut down truth in the daily decisions we make. He will encourage us to be stuck in shame and unforgiveness. He'll trivialize grace and whisper that we should hold grudges and never forget offenses. He entices us through the open door of destructive relationships and habits. He feeds our greed and makes us slaves to excess.

In Matthew 13 when Jesus talks about the parable of the seeds, He says Satan exploits a lack of understanding. He can snatch out the seed of truth before it can take root. Satan's ways do not always involve obvious sabotage.

Also recognize that while you're uncovering the plans of the enemy, not everything is warfare. Every red light is not an attack of Satan. Just because you have all green lights on the way to work does not mean the Lord is on your side. A good parking space is not necessarily a spiritual victory (although you're certainly welcomed to shout and do a quick fist pump). The aim is not to trivialize spiritual warfare but be aware that it's real and active. The truth is, sometimes you get a bad parking spot because it's Saturday and the store is crowded.

If your character or God's glory is not at stake, then just chalk it up to "life happens." If the outcome of a situation will impact how others think of God, how you love God, or how you love others, you're dealing with spiritual warfare. This is bigger than hindering personal convenience or achieving your own goals. For example, when I interact with my husband or someone who's close to me and they say something that touches on an issue that I haven't released them from yet, the way I respond in that next moment is critical as it determines whether or not God will be glorified. It impacts how I love that person. Will I choose sacrificial love or self-centeredness? In those moments, I choose sacrificial love (I wish those moments were more frequent), I know God is at work when my mouth opens with *wisdom and kindness* (Proverbs 31:26) rather than defensiveness and sarcasm.

Another area where God's glory is at stake is in the way I spend my money. When I actually need (not want) something and a gift card shows up for what I need or what I need suddenly becomes available at a greatly reduced price - that's spiritual. God is making provision. On the flip side when God is challenging me to spend my money the way He says to spend it, it's no accident that the clothes/car/things for my kids, etc. suddenly cross my path for a price I know I shouldn't pay. Neither of these instances are coincidental. There are plenty of things we might chalk up lightheartedly to some kind of spiritual warfare while other things are too quickly dismissed.

You have to be aware. You cannot afford to be clueless. Know it's there whether or not you choose to see it.

In 1 Peter 5:8 we learn we are to be sober-minded. Basically, be on alert so you don't get swept up into evil schemes – regardless of how subtle they are. Being on alert requires that my mind be more concerned with spiritual things than earthly things. If I fight this battle in the spiritual realm, then that's where my mind needs to be.

Concerns like marital status, marital happiness, the success of your kids, how much weight you need to lose, the person that has hurt you, when you're going to finish school, or when you're going to get your next promotion, keep your mind tethered to earth. It's easy to be so preoccupied with what we want that we miss what's happening in the spiritual realm.

Do you know how easy it is to miss the spiritual activity happening around us each day? So many things that we spend our time and attention on are the things that we can see and touch. It's not the person who we can see and touch that we need to be concerned with in most cases; it's the thing happening in the spirit that's driving our encounters. If we don't wage war in the spirit, we'll find ourselves stuck living a life in the flesh that God never intended for us. In fighting the spiritual war, we need to become educated and familiar with the weapons of warfare. There are some good things that we can do to equip ourselves to prepare for this spiritual battle. It's time to prepare. We need to educate ourselves on our adversary, our armor, and the arsenal our God has given us.

Are you ready? Maybe not now, but keep reading. You will be.

THREE

YOUR ADVERSARY, YOUR ARMOR, AND YOUR ARSENAL

"For the weapons of our warfare are not of the flesh but have divine power to destroy strongholds."
(2 Corinthians 10:4)

The battleground is undefined. The enemy is unseen.

When we choose to engage in spiritual battle the cloud of the unknown always hangs above us. There are always questions, uncertainties, and insecurities as we rely on God to give us guidance. However, we can do our part in minimizing those insecurities. We start by understanding our adversary, Satan. He is a real enemy and with real plans for our destruction. There are so many *places* Satan may attack - work, home, in our car, even at church! Not only that, there are so many *ways* he may strike. Through friends, family, finances, the list goes on. Those are two big unknowns. But what we can know, and are held responsible for, is knowing our enemy and knowing our weapons. The enemy may be unseen but he is not unknown. The battleground may be undefined but our weapons are not unknown.

Look back at 2 Corinthians 10:4 - *For the weapons of our warfare are not of the flesh but have divine power to destroy strongholds.* That verse is packed full of information but we're going to focus on these "*weapons*" that have "*divine power.*" These weapons are clearly not of the flesh but are of the Spirit of God. Understand that a weapon is not limited to an offensive tool. It can be defined as anything that provides an advantage – be it offensive or defensive. According to Ephesians 6, our armor and our arsenal are the divine weapons at our disposal. We may not know the plan of the enemy's attack or the place of the enemy's attack but we can understand the enemy's approach, put on the armor of God, and go into battle with divine weapons.

Ephesians 6:11-18 states:

> 11 Put on the whole armor of God, that you may be able to stand against the schemes of the devil. 12 For we do not wrestle against flesh and blood, but against the rulers, against the authorities, against the cosmic powers over this present darkness, against the spiritual forces of evil in the heavenly places. 13 Therefore take up the whole armor of God, that you may be able to withstand in the evil day, and having done all, to stand firm. 14 Stand therefore, having fastened on the belt of truth, and having put on the breastplate of righteousness, 15 and, as shoes for your feet, having put on the readiness given by the gospel of peace. 16 In all circumstances take up the shield of faith, with which you can extinguish all the flaming

darts of the evil one; 17 and take the helmet of salvation, and the sword of the Spirit, which is the word of God, 18 praying at all times in the Spirit, with all prayer and supplication. To that end, keep alert with all perseverance, making supplication for all the saints,...

Let's look at two important aspects of this passage.

First - we need to understand the adversary, or enemy, we're fighting against, and second - we need to understand the weapons (arsenal and armor) with which we are fighting. How can we wage a war and be unaware of the adversary? How can we win a war and be ignorant of our weapons? We can't be blind on either front.

KNOW YOUR ADVERSARY

We'll start by getting a better understanding of our adversary. An army that goes into war without an understanding of the enemy it fights, yet expects victory,
is setting itself up for failure.

Here, Paul isn't encouraging you to start something with your enemy. He's equipping you to stand.

We start with Ephesians 6:11 which calls us to stand. Paul doesn't charge us to take the enemy captive or to go on the offensive and initiate a fight. He lays a groundwork before he explains the armor. He wants to make it clear that this divine armor helps us to resist the plans of the devil. Some of you, like me, are natural-born fighters and we are not afraid of a good confrontation – you may even thrive on it. Here, Paul isn't encouraging you to start something with your enemy. He's equipping you to stand firm. In order to stand firm, we must be prepared and ready, to the best of our ability, for Satan's attacks. For all the fighters out there, preparation and readiness are nothing to scoff at. Let's look at what we're up against.

Look at verse 12. It lines up perfectly with the truth in 2 Corinthians 10:4. It affirms that our fight is spiritual and goes on to give great detail about who our enemy is. We read that we fight *against the rulers, against the powers, against the world forces of this darkness, against the spiritual forces of this wickedness.* This is the real question. Why would we wage a war according to our flesh when the enemy is not of the flesh? We must follow the rules of the spiritual realm because the enemy is a spiritual enemy.

Notice all the titles and positions Paul lists? Do they matter? Actually, yes. If God put the details in His Word, they must serve a purpose. Let's try to understand the purpose.

...against the rulers,...

The idea of a *ruler* is a chief, a principal, or a leader, and this simply means to have a position of priority or preeminence. The enemy is not a random group of hit men waiting around the corner for you. Satan has a hierarchy. He has an organizational structure of evil that is planned and organized. Satan is thoughtful, strategic, and intentional. When Paul says "rulers," he's alluding to the hierarchy that exists in the kingdom of darkness. In the last chapter, we talked about Israel being attacked by Amalek, and we saw that it was a spiritual battle. The army of Amalek came and attacked Israel shortly after God had parted the Red Sea and right after God had brought manna down from heaven.

That was not just about flesh and blood; that was a spiritual attack. The Israelite army needed to be attacked, and Satan brought an army against them.

Take a look at the book of Daniel. Specifically, chapter 10, verse 13. In the midst of answering Daniel's prayer, Michael, the archangel, comes to him and says, "*I was on my way to you, but I had to wage war with the Prince of Persia.*" Here we see that there is an angelic force sitting over a particular region and there's a prince of darkness ruling. Since an angel was waging war, Satan sent an angel, or prince, as his representative. So we literally have an angel of light and an angel of darkness fighting a spiritual battle. Nothing like some good angel-to-angel combat to keep things exciting.

Let's break it down to a more personal level. When it comes to you, the enemy uses personalized weapons for your spiritual attack. In other words, person-to-person combat. It's no coincidence when sexual temptation comes wrapped in a package that appeals to you. It's not an accident when you encounter people who play on your insecurities and seek to capitalize on your fears. You may even find another Christ-follower who, intentionally or unintentionally, causes strife in your life.

The bottom line is this:

- If an army needs to be brought down, Satan's going to send an army.
- If an angel needs to be fought, he's going to send an angel.
- If an individual needs to be wrestled with, he's going to send another individual.

That is what he does. He strategizes and he plans. He delegates and he escalates depending on the goal he's trying to achieve. If the first thing doesn't work, he has a plan B, C, D, and so on.

...against the powers, against the world forces of darkness,...

Power points to authority. Paul makes it clear that Satan has authority. Although his authority is limited to what God has allowed, it does exist. So it's wasted prayers, breath, and energy to try and declare Satan powerless. He does have power. He doesn't have power over God's will, he doesn't have power over God, and he doesn't have to have power over you. But it will serve us well to be aware of the fact our adversary is not powerless.

The term *world forces of darkness* simply means a shadow. It's a metaphor describing the darkness and the evil of Satan's empire. Although the kingdom of darkness has been defeated for eternity because of the Cross, there is still the everyday battle that we have to face. The darkness doesn't always take on the image of doom and gloom and sadness. Darkness can creep in when we allow the light of Christ to be dimmed in our lives. We can easily subject ourselves to darkness when we don't stand firm. This can be the case when despair turns to depression. This gradual dimming or darkening of the mind can lead us down very dangerous paths – much like the friends I referenced at the beginning of this book. I know that as a believer heaven is a done deal. No take-backs. But that doesn't mean I'm not susceptible to the forces of darkness. That's the battle we face.

A while back, a movie called *The Devil's Advocate* was released. It was a fascinating movie and is still one of my favorite films. The storyline centers around a young attorney (or advocate) played by Keanu Reeves, who was very good at his job. He had an uncanny ability to select juries, thereby increasing his success rate in court. At one point in the story, the attorney had a choice to make. Would he represent a man he believed to be guilty of child molestation? Would he choose honesty and jeopardize his career?

The movie follows a path based on the attorney making the dishonest choice. Initially, it looked like there would be only good consequences for his choice. He's offered a better job, better money, and a better house. The plot took an interesting twist as the young attorney's wife began to suffer from severe depression and he was presented with more opportunities to be deceptive and immoral. The story took another unexpected turn when the leader of the new firm, played by Al Pacino, who offered this "better life," revealed his dark side. Many visuals representing spiritual darkness were used to convey Pacino was much more than a greedy or unkind man. He had powers of darkness at his beck and call to accomplish his plans. All of this came to a head (spoiler alert!) when the young attorney's wife commits suicide.

So the viewer thinks.

A few moments later, we are clued into the fact this was all a dream of *what could have been.* What?! I know. I know! Actually, I felt relieved because the intensity took my emotions on a roller coaster ride. The final scenes went back in time and showed the young attorney, back in his small town with his wife, having just won a big case. You breathe a sigh of relief, glad that he made the right choice of humility rather than vanity. But wait, it's not over. As he's leaving the courthouse, a reporter says, "Are you sure you're not going to let me interview you? This is amazing!" He thought about it and reminded the reporter this case wasn't about him and he didn't do interviews. The reporter begged and convinced Reeves of how monumental this case was and it needed to be shared with the world. After a short hesitation, Reeves

Even though the devil couldn't trip him up with blatant darkness of dishonesty, he could trip him up with subtle shadows of vanity.

finally says, "Call me in the morning." The camera pans to the reporter as he celebrates his accomplishment and in a matter of seconds, the reporter's face morphs into the face of Al Pacino. In that moment we saw that even though the devil couldn't trip him up with the blatant darkness of dishonesty, he could trip him up with subtle shadows of vanity. We saw an enemy who was relentless and always attacking.

One good decision doesn't buy you rest or give you a reason to let your guard down. The enemy will adjust his strategy as needed in order to influence you with his darkness. We must be on the lookout for his subtle attempts at every turn.

If you ever find yourself thinking and acting under the dark influences of sin and you're wondering *How did I get here?*, the answer is always the same. One step at a time. The first step is not always a leap. Sometimes the first step is a baby step. The enemy doesn't care how big of a step you take. He has a goal, and he doesn't care how you reach it. Even if you are a follower of Jesus, you are still subject to the influence of the kingdom of darkness.

> When we choose not to obey truth, not to surrender to Jesus Christ, it automatically puts us in a realm that we're not supposed to be in. We immediately suffer the consequences of the evil one who has authority in the sphere of darkness.
>
> —Wayne Barber

Every choice you make either aligns you with the kingdom of

light or the kingdom of darkness. You don't have to be a devil worshiper to be influenced by the schemes of the devil. If you don't think you're susceptible, you're an accident waiting to happen. Stay on guard. There is a powerful enemy and he has plans for you.

...against spiritual forces of wickedness....

Here Paul shifts from the power and plans of the enemy to addressing the practices of the kingdom of darkness. Wickedness points to depravity. In essence, when we are influenced by darkness, we act wickedly. This shows itself when we are hurt and offended by the sinful actions of others. Don't be deceived, your boss is not the enemy. Your spouse isn't either (no really, I've looked into this). Our ex-whatever isn't the enemy - stop plotting! The enemy isn't our mother, father, or our siblings. If we can see it or touch it, it's not the enemy. If someone has ill intent, ill motives, seeks to cause us harm, hurt us, or brings a hindrance, it is wickedness. The "spiritual forces of wickedness" are at work. It may be wickedness wrapped up in the godliest person we know. It doesn't matter, because all it takes is for one person's vulnerability and weakness to line up with the schemes of the enemy, and before we know it, wickedness wins in that moment.

I know what you may be thinking. *I can steer clear of those types of situations, I won't let myself be vulnerable or susceptible to the enemy.* Let me gently stop you right there. Human wisdom is no match for spiritual wickedness. Our wisdom is not a "divine weapon" but it's a weapon of the flesh. It

Human wisdom is no match for spiritual wickedness.

serves no purpose in a spiritual battle. Human reasoning and rationale get us in more trouble than they get us out of. Just ask Eve. When Satan came to her with a proposition, she didn't say, "Hold on, let me talk to my husband. Or better yet, let me talk to God." Nope. She said, "Let me process this on my own." She used her own logic and decision-making skills to battle the devil. How did that work out? Not convinced? Let's check in with David. He was a pretty smart guy too. He was a warrior! He was a worshiper! In all of his wisdom, he let lust get the best of him. Then he plotted murder to cover up his adultery.

Two quick notes:

1. Being a warrior – an achiever – doesn't make you immune to wickedness.
2. Being a worshiper doesn't make you immune to wickedness.

The human wisdom approach didn't work out so well for Sarah either. She schemed about how to bring forth the child that God said *He* was going to bring forth through a miracle. Not only did human understanding fail Eve, David, and Sarah – they suffered significant and long lasting consequences. Yes they loved God, but they had moments where they loved their logic even more – and that opened the door to wickedness.

We often take lightly the power and the planning of the enemy. The Bible does not tell us about the enemy so we can be fearful, but so we can be alert. Only when you acknowledge the planning, power, and practices of the enemy can you begin to understand the weaponry that God has given you to fight him. You can know in your mind God is sovereign and victory is guaranteed.

Not only do we strengthen our standing by learning about our adversary, we do so by understanding our armor. Looking back at Ephesians 6:11, the only way we can withstand these schemes of the devil is to put on the full armor of God.

So what exactly is included in this package?

Belt of Truth

"...having fastened on the belt of truth,..." Ephesians 6:14

Paul compares the armor of God with military gear; each piece represents a part of God's strength that He extends to us when we become His children. Verse 14 gives us the first piece of armor – the belt of truth. Seems simple right? Yes, it's simple but it's also serious. The belt of a Roman soldier in Paul's day was not a simple leather strap such as we wear today. It was a thick, heavy leather and metal band with a protective piece hanging down from the front of it. The belt held the soldier's sword and other weapons.

The word *truth* means exposed, out in the open, or not hidden. In our context, truth means anything that has been revealed to us about God's nature and His character. What has God left out in the open for us to know? That's the truth we must pursue – and it's all in His Word. See, truth is not a moving target; it's not relative. It's not related to culture, popular opinion, or pressure. What was true in the beginning, is true today, and will be true to the end. However, our culture likes a relative kind of truth. Just look around. What was once considered immodest or inappropriate is no longer so. Our society's standards on sexuality, violence, greed, etc. are on a sliding scale. What's true for one person is not considered true for all. But God isn't concerned about truth determined by our culture. He's only concerned about absolute, divine truth. In other words, His truth. Don't forget, the enemy thrives on deception so he's naturally opposed to truth. The deception you buy into may be rooted in explicit evil or good intentions. It doesn't really matter. As long as it deviates from God's truth, the enemy is succeeding.

The deception you buy into may be rooted in explicit evil or good intentions.

Note Jesus' interaction with Peter in Matthew 16:21-23. Jesus is foretelling His death and resurrection. He tells his disciples that a time is coming when He will suffer, be killed, and be raised. Peter passionately opposes the Lord's prophecy and responds in kind. The Bible says Peter rebukes Jesus. In hindsight, that doesn't seem smart; but I'm sure in the moment Peter felt like it was the right thing to say. He had good intentions. But that's not how Jesus saw it because He responded harshly to Peter, in verse 23, by saying "*Get behind Me, Satan! You are a hindrance to me.*" Jesus didn't express his gratitude for Peter's passion or concern. He didn't empathize with his perspective. Instead He called him Satan. *Satan.* You might be thinking, *Okay Jesus, doesn't that seem a little harsh? I mean, it's Peter. Your number one follower (for the most part).* Peter may have had good intentions but he deviated from the truth because it wasn't what he wanted to believe or accept. Jesus didn't say those words because Peter was a follower of Satan, but because in that moment Peter was under the influence of Satan. Even with good intentions, Peter was contradicting the truth and in spiritual warfare, there's no room for that.

Truth can't be compromised.

When we gird ourselves with the belt of truth, it gives us the foundation of God's absolute standards. Truth cannot be compromised even if it doesn't feel good. As soon as we begin to contradict the truth, we begin moving under the influence of the kingdom of darkness. We have to faithfully hold the truth of God's Word and allow it to hold us. There are some lies we believe that make it difficult to cling to truth. This becomes critical when it comes to taking thoughts captive, because if we don't uproot the lies in our minds, then there is no room for the truth.

Everybody has some standard of what they call reality or truth. Basically, everybody has their perspective. Individualized truth and spirituality are prevalent in our culture today. Paul's mission here is to admonish us as believers to begin to replace whatever truth we have created for ourselves with God's truth. If we take an honest look within ourselves, we may discover thoughts that are more reflective or our individual perspective rather than God's universal truth. Thoughts like:

- *God isn't really good – therefore I need to be good to myself.*
- *God doesn't really love me - if He does, I have to earn it with good behavior.*
- *I'm not worthy – so I'll give myself away to anyone.*
- *God can't forgive me – I will be trapped by shame.*
- *God owes me – I will demand that He repays me with blessings and answered prayer.*

Sometimes, we don't utter blatant lies; we just express doubt about the truth. We begin to think that when we do something good, God owes us or we condemn ourselves for things He's forgiven. This is why it's critical to bear this in mind. Truth isn't based on personal perspective or individual experience. Those things make truth conditional and conditional truth is not truth at all. Truth has to be true all the time. God has to always be good. He has to always love you. He has to always be enough. If someone were to ask me, "Jada, are you a female?" I would answer yes. If someone asked, "Are you 5 foot 4?" Again, I would answer yes. (I would probably add that in my heels, I am 5 foot 8.) There are no conditions on that information. I am always female, 5 foot 4, the wife of Conway, the mother of our son Joah, born in Dallas, and a lover of Jesus Christ. It doesn't matter the circumstances under which someone is asking me those questions. The answers given are just true. They are unconditional.

On the other hand, I could turn around and say, I really love summer. I love to travel and going to the beach. Pizza is my favorite comfort food. While those are things that are generally true about me, they're not unconditionally true. I don't love summer if it's too hot. I don't love to travel if it becomes too inconvenient, and I don't particularly love the beach during a hurricane. And on rare occasions, I actually don't want pizza. But general truth doesn't work with God. God's truth is unconditional.

Have you fallen victim to a sliding scale of truth?

Have you fallen victim to a sliding scale of truth? Think about it. Can you back up your beliefs with God's truth? Do your decisions depend on what God has to say? If we don't stay rooted in truth, we'll get swept away by our reasoning and emotions.

When you're working harder on your marriage by talking to your husband as opposed to being on your knees, you're believing that God cannot hear you and make a change unless your mouth is open. That's a lie you believe about God. When you're unmarried and you've been celibate for ten years, you might think that surely this one time God can understand that you have needs. You may begin to believe that God doesn't want consistent righteousness, but that He'll give you credit, and that He's going to forgive you because you need to be happy. You can convince yourself that God "understands."

When I make decisions that are outside of God's plan for me, I promise you, they are always fueled by a lie, and they have to be countered with what is true. I have to believe that God loves me enough that if I am not married and I am fifty-five, it is not punishment; it is not a lack of God's love. If I am married and I'm twenty-five, and I can't believe I'm going to be here the rest of my life, it's still not punishment; God loves me the same. If I cannot afford a house and I'm forty and I always thought I'd be in a house and I'm still in an apartment, God is still my provider. He's no more a provider when I close on my house than when I sign my apartment agreement. See, truth is truth no matter the circumstances.

If you're going to have a belt of truth that you constantly take off and put on, you're not going to be able to wage war. You won't always have a warning before the adversary attacks. You have to put on the belt of truth and keep it on, and it has to be unconditional and absolutely hang on the truth that God's character doesn't change. When the weather changes and the circumstances change, God's character doesn't change. When your mood changes, when you feel different about God, when you respond differently to God, it's not because God has changed, it's because a lie has taken root in your mind, and you've chosen to believe that lie over the truth.

The truth is easy to embrace when it makes me feel good. But truth is truth no matter how it makes me feel. That's why weddings and funerals happen on the same day. In a NICU (Neonatal Intensive Care Unit) on any given day one baby lives and one baby dies. The same God oversees it all. He gives and takes away. Blessed be the name of the Lord (Job 1:21).

Paul says we have to embrace truth. We have to understand that it is a weapon. Warren Wiersbe said, "*Unless we are motivated and directed by truth, we will be defeated by the enemy. If we permit any deception into our lives, we have weakened our position, and cannot fight the battle victoriously.*" The belt of truth is not an offensive weapon, but it is one for protection. It does not prevent attacks, but it keeps the believer from being harmed by them.

When I'm rooted in truth, and Satan throws lies at me, I can counter those lies. If the truth I believe is unconditional, it's as true on a bad day when I don't feel super spiritual as it is on a day when I think I'm holy. Why is this? Because it's the truth of God.

Without truth we'll be on the path toward chaotic thoughts, not captive ones.

Breastplate of Righteousness

"...having put on the breastplate of righteousness,..." Ephesians 6:14

The next piece of armor we put on as we prepare for battle is the breastplate of righteousness. A typical soldier wore a breastplate made of bronze or chain mail. It covered the vital organs, namely, the heart, and was fitted with loops or buckles that attached it to a thick belt. If the belt (*of truth*) was loosened, the breastplate slipped right off.

This makes sense with the image Paul gives us because the righteousness represented by the breastplate is not the righteousness of salvation and eternity; that's secured. That is called *positional righteousness.* Here, Paul is talking about *practiced righteousness.*

Those in Christ already have positional righteousness so we don't have to "put on" the righteousness of salvation because that would imply it could be taken off. The righteousness given to us at salvation is secure and nothing can take it away. In 2 Corinthians 5:21, we read, "He made Him who knew no sin to become sin on my behalf, so that we might become the righteousness of God in Him." Second Corinthians 5:21 and Philippians 3:8-9 both reference positional righteousness.

This is not about trying to gain righteousness for ourselves. We gained it when we accepted His Son, Jesus Christ, as our Savior. The breastplate of righteousness is about practicing it. It means that we are to be conformed to an authoritative standard or norm of what God deems as "right." We have been given Christ's righteousness so that our eternity is secure, but we still have to practice that righteousness in our everyday lives. The Bible is clear that this is at the heart of Christian living:

> Blessed are those who hunger and thirst for righteousness, for they shall be satisfied. (Matthew 5:6)
>
> Present yourselves as alive to God and as instruments of righteousness. (Romans 6:13)

All of these truths work together in what Paul is calling us to do in 2 Corinthians, chapter 10.

The important thing to keep in mind about the standard of righteousness is it's just like God's truth, unconditional and unmoving. Righteousness is God's idea, not yours. Our thoughts and actions are either righteous or unrighteous. Satan, your adversary, would love to convince you that you can be "sort of" righteous. Don't fall for that argument; it's a lie and goes against the truth of God. We get into trouble when we begin to operate out of our own idea of righteousness. We rationalize our overspending if we are tithers and minimize our bad attitudes if we "meant well." We trivialize gossip and blur the line of ethics that honor Christ. We have to understand righteousness is not measured on good intentions or strong effort. God expects complete, not partial righteousness. Total stewardship that honors God is the goal, not simply tithing. Loving others according to 1 Corinthians 13, not merely keeping our negative words inside is the goal.

The breastplate of righteousness is about laying claim to Christ's righteousness, not creating our own.

The breastplate of righteousness is about laying claim to Christ's righteousness, not creating our own. Even though you are a believer, you're going to find times when you are filled with doubt, and the joy starts to fade because walking with Christ is a series of mountains and valleys. It will get discouraging, and sometimes you're going to have great days and great seasons, and sometimes you won't. There will be times when you feel free with your testimony and all that God has allowed in your life, and there will be other times when the shame is so heavy, you don't want to look anybody in the eye because if they see you, they're going to know what you have done. They're going to know your story; they're going to know what you've been through. There are times when the guilt just drives you, and all the heaviness seems to outweigh all the good.

It is in those moments you must remind yourself this breastplate of righteousness is not about you claiming your own qualification. It is about you hiding behind the protective righteousness of Jesus Christ. Only in Him do we even have a chance of yielding to the Spirit so we can walk in God's righteousness. Only when He has covered us with perfect righteousness can we confidently battle with the flesh and the Spirit.

When we think we've lost favor with God that speaks more about what we think of God than it does about what we think of ourselves. We begin to think God is flaky and He's conditional and that we have to be right for Him to love us. And that's not who He is. We must learn that this righteousness is not something we are building on our own. The breastplate of righteousness prepares us for battle because it gives the adversary fewer opportunities to trip us up. The more I pursue daily righteousness, the less likely I am to be deceived by my enemy and false ideas of righteousness. Do you know how to spot counterfeit currency? It's not by exposing yourself to the countless iterations of counterfeit money circulating in the economy. The only way to truly spot a counterfeit is to be so clear on what the real thing looks like any deviation from it is easily recognized. The same is true for our righteousness. We put on the breastplate of righteousness when we are so confident and consistent with God's standard of righteous living that any counterfeit is quickly noticed and resisted. Will you choose light or darkness? Sometimes we'll choose darkness, but the Holy Spirit will take us back. Sometimes we'll choose light, and we'll learn from it. At any rate, we've got the breastplate of righteousness covering us as we try to make our way toward the heart of God.

If we want to do battle in the Spirit, we must first be founded in the truth, and then we have to protect our hearts with righteousness.

Shoes of Peace

"...and, as shoes for your feet, having put on the readiness given by the gospel of peace." Ephesians 6:15

The third piece of armor is a very important pair of shoes. Roman soldiers had specially designed sandals that provided them with better traction so they could stand firm when they were being attacked. The word *readiness* implies constant vigilance. A victorious soldier had to be prepared for battle. He had to have studied his enemy's strategy, be confident in his own strategy, and have his feet firmly planted so that he could hold his ground when the attacks came. A soldier's battle shoes were studded with nails or spikes, like cleats, to help him keep his balance in combat. He knew that if he lost his footing and went down, it wouldn't matter how great the rest of his armor was; the enemy had him. When we are ready with the gospel of peace, we live with the understanding that we are continually under attack from Satan but we rest on the peace we have in the Gospel. The word *gospel* simply means good news; it means a good message. The gospel of peace is a specific kind of good news. It conveys the idea that God has already fully reconciled man to Himself. The word peace here means *to bring back or join together that which was once divided.* So God has already brought about peace where we had division.

This is such an important truth to understand. Paul expands on this idea in 2 Corinthians 5:17-18 and 21.

> 17 Therefore, if anyone is in Christ, he is a new creation. The old has passed away; behold, the new has come. 18 All this is from God, who through Christ reconciled us to himself;... 21 For our sake he made him to be sin who knew no sin, so that in him we might become the righteousness of God.

What the enemy will seek to do is to bring division and chaos into our lives, and we will run from peace and embrace strife and misery and miss the whole idea of this weapon. This gospel is good news because while we were still sinners, God came after us and brought us peace.

According to 2 Corinthians 5, He gave us the ministry of reconciliation, and Jesus sought to make things right when we could not do so on our own. He made the first move and will have the final move. Now that is good news! We have a certainty and a stability knowing that nothing can snatch us out of the hands of God. When the enemy brings whatever he has planned, we can stand firm on the foundation of the good news that Jesus Christ has already reconciled with us. There's not any decision or choice we can make that would take away that peace.

He made the first move and will have the final move. Now that is good news!

Some days I find myself wrestling with inner turmoil. We all have days like that when we just want things to settle down. It seems like there's always a million things going through our minds. There seems to always be a thousand problems that need to be solved. It can feel like there are more questions than answers. But no one knows the inner turmoil we're going through. We will be sitting quietly, and on the outside we look like we have it together, but on the inside we're shaken up. We don't have a sense of peace because the enemy has shaken our foundation. This is how despair turns to depression. This is the place that our hearts and insecurities begin to speak louder than God's truth and we must be careful not to listen. To quiet those lies, we are compelled to hold tightly to these truths:

- *God is at peace with me.*
- *There is no war outside of me that can conquer the peace that God has already given me.*
- *If God is my stability, then there's nothing the enemy can bring my way that should cause chaos or undo the unity and the peace that God has already given me.*

Don't let the enemy raise questions in your mind about things God already answered. Don't let him stir up turmoil when God has already granted peace. The devil wants you to think that on a "bad" day you are not loved by God. He wants your mind to spend its energy trying to *win* God's grace rather than walking in it toward righteousness.

When we prepare our feet with the gospel of peace, we can take a promise from eternity and apply it to earth and let that be our stabilizing force as we do battle. We don't wrestle against men and women, bosses and co-workers, family and friends, or flesh and blood. There is an organized adversary with whom we wrestle. He has rulers, princes, armies, and angels working on his behalf. This enemy is serious and he has a plan for us. But God has a greater plan. If we would take up the belt of truth, if we would take up the breastplate of righteousness, and prepare ourselves with the firm foundation of the gospel of peace, we are halfway through equipping ourselves to wage war with the enemy.

Shield of Faith

"In all circumstances take up the shield of faith, with which you can extinguish all the flaming darts of the evil one." Ephesians 6:16

What's interesting about this particular piece of armor is it's the first one in which Paul explains how it will be used. He says you will use the shield of faith to extinguish the flaming darts, or missiles that the evil one is going to launch your way.

What kind of super shield is this exactly? The image is of a traditional gladiator's shield. If you've seen the movie *300*, you'll notice there are two kinds of shields used during battle. There's the small circular shield that allows you to run and be mobile while you fight. It protects a specific portion of the body and is usually about two and half feet in diameter. Then there's the full body shield similar to what you see in the movie *Braveheart*. Those shields were usually about five feet tall and were pitched deeply into the ground. You didn't carry them to go attack your enemy; you just hid behind them until the enemy got close enough to engage in combat. This is the kind of shield that's being described here. Paul is giving us a visual image of the shield we'll need as we engage in spiritual warfare.

Up until this point, we have the belt of truth holding everything together, the gospel of peace as our foundation, and covering our heart is the breastplate of righteousness. With truth, peace, and righteousness we stand behind the shield of faith. According to Hebrews 11:1, faith is defined as assurance and conviction.

"Now faith is the assurance of things hoped for, the conviction of things not seen." (Hebrews 11:1)

As believers, we have full conviction, certainty, and confidence in the work, Word, and will of God. This shield of faith protects truth, peace, and righteousness in our hearts. If that shield is weak, and our faith gets shaky, we are prone to not live in truth, peace, or righteousness. We are more susceptible to the flaming arrows of lies, chaos, temptation, and sin. We wrestle with the deception of the enemy and of our flesh. We struggle with inner turmoil because we doubt God's peace. And ultimately our behavior follows our beliefs into a pit of unrighteousness. On the other hand, when our faith is strong it doesn't matter what the enemy brings our way. Our faith can extinguish all the other things he's trying to attack behind the shield.

When we're secured by truth, covered in the righteousness of Christ, and standing behind the shield of faith, we don't have to throw caution to the wind or just cross our fingers and hope it's going to work. It is guaranteed that faith always thwarts the plan of the enemy. Always. Faith works every single time. As we look back on our own lives when the enemy has been successful, I can promise you it was coupled with a lack of faith. Not sometimes; every single time. Our minds become so chaotic we're no longer certain about the God in whom we believe – that is the essence of losing faith. We leave our confidence in God on the floor and don't take it with us out the door. It's not a Sunday confidence. It's an everyday conviction that strengthens us as we do battle. This issue of faith is so important to our success in this spiritual war. If you look through the gospels, the lack of faith was the only thing for which Jesus consistently rebuked the disciples. He knew, and emphasized to them, faith would make or break them on this journey of life. In a strange way, it's comforting that Jesus is most concerned about my faith because that's something I know I can control. I won't be the most gifted or the most knowledgeable. But the amount of faith that I choose to walk with is entirely up to me.

So here's the image. You're behind this shield of faith and the enemy has some supernatural archer's bow, and he is shooting these flaming arrows at you. What kinds of things are considered *flaming darts*?

The flaming arrows are things that produce opportunities for our flesh to be enticed toward unrighteousness. Temptations, such as impurity, lust, greed, vanity, materialism, pride, anger, impatience, jealousy, and envy are common arrows the adversary aims at us. The enemy does not want us to ever be satisfied, content, sure, or certain. The things that he's going to shoot our way are going to be temptations that change our thinking from the certainty, hope, promise, and abundance of Jesus Christ to the doubt, despair, and discouragement that happens when we get stuck on the things of this earth.

As we look through the book of Job, which gives us one of the clearest examples of Satan having to get permission from God to test His servant, we see a physical test with a spiritual lesson.

God might allow a physical circumstance in your life in order to teach a spiritual lesson. When God brought Job full circle, Job didn't say, "I'm so glad that I have all of my things back." Job said, "*I have heard of You by the hearing of the ear; But now my eye sees You*" (Job 42:5). When God stripped all the physical stuff away, Job realized he wasn't as faithful as he thought he was. He might have thought a little too highly of himself, as we do, only to realize his love for God was connected to his wealth, health, and family. Taking those things away gave him an opportunity to see what he really thought about God.

The ultimate goal of the enemy is always to unsettle the mind. That's why Paul is going to tell us again in 2 Corinthians 10 that those thoughts have to be taken captive because that's what the enemy is after: your mind. The enemy is not just randomly shooting those flaming darts into the air hoping they're going to hit their target. He's strategic, organized, and intentional. God has a plan for your life, and so does your adversary.

First John 2:16 says, "For all that is in the world, the lust of the flesh and the lust of the eyes and the boastful pride of life, is not from the Father, but is from the world." The darts that the enemy is going to throw your way are meant to connect with one of those three things. He is going to throw things that stir up the lust of the flesh, the lust of the eyes, or the pride of life (or all of the above). When you fall and make bad decisions, it's not because the devil made you do it. It's because the devil suspected you wanted to do it, and he gave you an opportunity, and you gave in. When he shoots the dart of jealousy your way, it connects with that lust of the flesh or that pride of life. When he aims the dart of greed at you, the lust of the eyes and flesh invite you to spend beyond your means. Then you find yourself having to wrestle with decisions because you yielded to the desires of your flesh. It's the same thing that Satan got Eve with (Genesis 3). It's the same thing that happened with Samson and Delilah (Judges 16), and with David and Bathsheba (2 Samuel 4). There was something in the flesh, a sexual need, the lust of the flesh and the lust of the eyes. Let's take a closer look.

Lust of the flesh is simply the craving of the body. Physical cravings of the body that might be otherwise legitimate can turn out to be evil because they're being used for self-fulfillment and not for God's glory. Satan takes things that are good and works them into evil. It's okay to be hungry, but he got Eve thinking, that his idea was a good choice. She let her flesh and basic feeling of hunger influence her decisions. There was nothing wrong with hunger, but God had already made provision for how to satisfy that hunger. There's nothing wrong with having a relationship with a woman, but David knew it needed to be with his wife and not another man's wife. The same goes for Samson and Delilah.

The **lust of the eyes** is the desire to possess what we see. We live in a society where we always talk about men being visual. You know they love their cars, their possessions, and their women; but women are visual too. We love beauty. We have a thing with vanity. We love to shop. Women spend quite a bit of time and money on things that effect our image. Hair, makeup, and clothes get top priority for many of us (it's no secret that most women dress for other women). Keeping our kids shiny and homes immaculate are also lofty goals we often set for ourselves. Then of course there are the gym memberships, supplement purchases, boot camps. Yeah, yeah, I know you do it for your health. That's why all my friends post "before and after" pictures of their organs and xrays – so we can all see how their health improved. Seriously, we post picture of our weight loss and body improvements because women are visual and are driven by beauty.

I remember when Conway and I visited some friends for dinner. Their house was simply breathtaking. I walked in and felt like I was in a magazine. The kitchen was life-changing. The artwork and design were gorgeous. The outdoor kitchen/entertainment area was the icing on the cake. We had a great time at dinner - good food and good conversation. As we got in the car to head home, several hours later, the first thing out of my mouth was "We need a new house!" Conway and I both burst out laughing because we knew we had some serious house envy. Even after we got back home, I looked around and felt dissatisfied with our house. I had to make a shift from grumbling to gratitude, and shake off the lust that had started with my eyes, so I could appreciate the home God has blessed us with.

You see that in Genesis 3. Not only was Eve hungry, but the fruit was beautiful to her eyes. The fruit was nice to look at. Women are concerned about the presentation of food. Men want to consume food. The enemy uses that against us to tempt us toward false thoughts and unhealthy thinking.

The pride of life is anything that exalts us and offers an illusion of God. Pride is a sneaky thing. You don't have to go around beating your chest and telling everybody you're the greatest to show that you struggle with pride. It's a guarantee that our flesh is geared toward self-elevation, and that's what pride is. Pride can show itself in so many forms. It can make you think, you can figure things out on your own. When I'm asking God for something and I'm waiting, and waiting, and waiting, pride sabotages my patience. It may lead me to take matters into my own hands like Moses did (Exodus 2:11-12) or Sarah (Genesis 16).

What happens when I'm waiting but then He answers somebody else's prayer before He answers mine? Do I keep waiting? Or do I begin thinking maybe that's a sign from God saying I need to take the initiative? You know how we spiritualize things. That's what happens when we subject ourselves to the pride of life: in subtle ways, we start to convince ourselves that we know better than God. And it's the same thing that gets us every single time. The enemy throws these darts at our shield of faith and if our shield is weak we'll get hit. The shield of faith isn't used effectively simply because we attend church or possess a Bible or Bible app. This shield is only effective based on the assurance and conviction we have about God's truth. Warren Wiersbe, one of my favorite Bible commentators, says, "*If these fiery darts aren't extinguished by faith, they will ignite whatever they touch, and then we have a destructive fire to put out.*"

Satan can throw the fiery dart of doubt our way if he knows we are struggling with the lust of the flesh, the lust of the eyes, and the pride of life. When those darts connect, they start fires in the flesh that manifest in doubt or disbelief in God (the opposite of faith).

For example, consider a woman who is questioning whether or not she's going to get married. She may have tried to emotionally separate herself and dismiss the idea because she's a strong personality, a certain age, too successful, or has a child. If she dwells on the possibility of this desire not being met, she will have a hard time standing firmly behind her shield of faith. Then when her lack of faith in God's goodness or His plan for her life gets shaky, it impacts how she relates to men. She may participate in a relationship with a man who is not a Christ follower. This woman could give in to desires of the flesh through sexual and emotional intimacy with a man that isn't her husband. Her friendships with other women could become strained because she's unable to celebrate the marriages of others. All this because of weak faith.

Satan can take one dart, one fiery missile, and when it connects to a place where my faith is weak, it will spread like wildfire in my life. When he throws fear my way, if I'm already insecure or discontent, with what God has/has not given me, I can't relate to people in a loving way and I'll end up being nasty sometimes. More importantly, I allow these thoughts of discontentment to take root in my mind and cause chaos.

We can't allow a fiery dart to hit the weak point in our shield of faith and cause a wildfire. Rest assured, the devil can't keep you out of heaven once you choose Jesus. All he can do is render you ineffective while you're here on earth. He can't change eternity. He's not necessarily trying to take you out. He knows he can't keep you out of heaven, but he can do enough damage to distract you and derail you from God's mission. Will you stand behind that shield of faith?

Helmet of Salvation

"and take the helmet of salvation..." Ephesians 6:17

The helmet of salvation is next up in our battle preparation. A helmet covers the head of the soldier and protects his brain. The helmet of salvation protects the soldier's mind with the knowledge that he/she possesses about the truth of God's salvation. It's not about being saved, because this armor is for the person who's already a believer. It's about the future hope that we have in Jesus Christ's return.

John MacArthur says it this way: *"There are three aspects to salvation. There's the past - we've been saved from the penalty of sin. The present - we've been saved from the power of sin. In the future - we've been saved from the presence of sin."*

The helmet of salvation is the believer's hope in the future.

The helmet of salvation is the believer's hope in the future. It's the idea that I believe that not only has God saved me for my time here, but Jesus Christ is going to return, and there's going to be a day when all of this warfare will cease. I must live with that hope, otherwise I will allow what's happening around me to define my reality. I have to live with a future-minded perspective. That's what the helmet of salvation does. It keeps Satan from using discouragement and hopelessness as weapons against us.

Discouragement can even hit God's leaders. If you read the stories of Moses and Elijah, both of them, at some point, became so discouraged they asked God to kill them. They loved God, and they were called by God, but they became discouraged. Hopelessness is the essence of depression. It's a real struggle. I know from statistics that probably half of the people reading this book have experienced depression firsthand or have seen someone that's one degree removed from depression. Hopelessness is one of the weapons that the enemy uses against us. Satan wants us to forget that he's been defeated for eternity. He wants us to forget that God is a promise keeper. The adversary's goal is to get you to focus on the "right now." He wants you to be short-sided and think more about earth than eternity. Our insta-society draws us into desire for immediate gratification. We throw things out into the social media universe and expect a boomerang of "likes," "comments," and "followers." But God has a different perspective. The Bible says in Matthew 16:25, "If you lose your life for My sake, then you'll have life." You need to have a perspective based on the helmet of salvation that assures you of salvation from the past and from the power of sin, but we've also been saved from the presence of sin forevermore. Once our time on this earth is over—and it is short—forever will be longer than the time we spend on earth. We'll be in a place where there will be no more sin and the enemy will have no more power.

Revelation 21:4 says, "*He will wipe away every tear from their eyes, and death shall be no more, neither shall there be mourning, nor crying, nor pain anymore, for the former things have passed away.*" The helmet of salvation is really about hope. It's about understanding that we don't need to see it in front of us right now, by faith, we know that one day all of this will end. If we know that it's going to end, and that in the end we win, then the enemy can't distract us when it seems like we're losing a little bit of ground. Even when we fail—because we're going to fail, fall short, and mess up—we know we can get back up, repent, find conviction, and keep moving forward in the Lord. The helmet of salvation is what gives us a hope that there is something much more powerful beyond what we're in today. It gives us the proper perspective and points to something greater. With this piece of armor, we can allow life to ebb and flow with both tragic loss and significant triumph without being defined by either.

When you leave this earth these things that can consume your thoughts won't even be relevant anymore. You're going to have a future with Jesus Christ in heaven for eternity where all of this is going to be irrelevant and nobody is going to care how many pairs of shoes you had, where you lived, how long your marriage lasted, how great your kids turned out, how much weight you actually lost, whether your husband treated you the way you wanted him to, or whether you were able to stay single and satisfied.

The hope of salvation is the thing that keeps us centered and focused on the future so the things of the present don't weigh us down. We have to deal with the present. We can't ignore it. It's real. It's there, but it cannot be the all consuming, defining reality of the believer because the believer, at salvation, was seated in heavenly places. We have to have a heavenly mindset if we're going to deal with earthly things in a way that pleases God. If we're as consumed with the earth as everybody else, then what in the world would entice someone to choose Jesus?

The Sword of the Spirit

"...and [take] the sword of the Spirit, which is the word of God..."
Ephesians 6:17

Remember we are strengthening our faith by learning about our adversary and understanding our armor. Now it's time to become familiar with our arsenal. When we think of an arsenal we probably will imagine a room with wall-to-wall weaponry; a place full of every kind of weapon imaginable. Well, what we're dealing with isn't exactly wall-to-wall options. We have one weapon in our entire arsenal. It's the only weapon we need because it always works. That is the sword of the Spirit. In Ephesians 6, it's the only offensive weapon we carry. This sword is not like one of those long swords you see or a fencing sword where you can maintain a distance and just swing and hope to hit something. It's a short dagger. The word used for sword here is a two-edged dagger which requires a lot of precision and skill in its use. You had to be pretty bold in battle to use this type of sword because it meant you're okay with the enemy being close to you so the metaphor Paul uses is very fitting.

Roman soldiers spent quite a bit of time perfecting the practice of this kind of dagger. It's a very specific tool used for precision cutting. You see a clear parallel to the word of God in Hebrews 4:12:

> For the word of God is living and active, sharper than any two-edged sword, piercing to the division of soul and of spirit, of joints and of marrow, and discerning the thoughts and intentions of the heart. (ESV)

You're going to need to understand God's Word and use it with precision so that you will be able to slice through the lies and the falsehood that the devil is going to bring your way. How many times has the enemy come at you through another individual, or through a certain situation, and you were ill-equipped? You have the power to control that. It doesn't have to be that way; you can equip yourself with the Word of God. You have to take up the sword of the Spirit. You have to take the Word of God seriously.

What is your skill level with the sword of the Spirit? What do you really know? In battle there's not time to go and borrow someone else's sword. When the enemy comes your way you shouldn't have to go to your mother, friend, or your pastor. You'll want to quote the living, breathing Word of God because that's the only thing that sends the enemy running. It's the Word of God. Not your good ideas, not your good points, not even good sermon notes.

In Matthew, chapter 4, we find a perfect example of Jesus using the Word of God when He was faced with temptation while in the wilderness on His forty-day fast. Starting with verse 3, we read, "*And the tempter came to Him and said, 'If You are the Son of God, command that these stones become bread.'* " Satan is trying to tempt Jesus with the lust of the flesh. The tempter knows Jesus is hungry. He knows that Jesus is also fully human. He's fully man even though He's fully God. His body's going to want food. Jesus responds in verse 4, "*It is written, 'man shall not live on bread alone, but on every word that proceeds out of the mouth of God.'* " That's it. He just quoted the Scripture and moved on. He didn't add to it or expand it.

You don't ever need to add to or defend God's Word. The enemy is not impressed with your opinions, declarations, or your long prayers. The only thing that sends him running is the absolute truth found in the Word of God. In verse 5, we read: "*The devil took Him to the holy city and had Him stand on the pinnacle of the temple.*" Now Satan tries to lure Jesus with the lust of the eyes. Satan says, to Him, " *'If You're the Son of God, throw Yourself down; for it is written, 'He will command His angels concerning You;' and 'on their hands they will bear You up, so You will not strike Your foot against a stone.'* " Yes, Satan knows the Scripture too.

In verse 7, Jesus responds with, '*On the other hand, it is written, "You shall not put the Lord your God to the test.'* " And in verse 8, it says, "*Again, the devil took Him to a very high mountain and showed Him all the kingdoms in the world...; and he said to Him, 'If You fall down and worship me I'll give You these things.' Then Jesus said to him, 'Go, Satan! For it is written, "You shall worship the Lord your God and serve Him only.'*" Every single time Satan brought something Jesus' way, Jesus used Scripture, the Word of God, as His answer.

That is what the power of the sword of the Spirit does. I think one of the mistakes that the church is making is that we have more access to the Word, but we have less application of the Word. We have more apps, more tools, more resources, Google, Bible websites, and more commentaries online—everything you could possibly need—but are often unable to articulate basic doctrine. Can you clearly explain the gospel and salvation to someone? Do you know why it's important that Jesus is fully God and fully man? How do you prove the existence of the Trinity?

Because we don't know, we sometimes make up our own truth. Have you heard any of these phrases?

- Cleanliness is next to godliness.
- If you take one step, God will take two.
- All things work together for good.
- God helps those who help themselves.
- Money is the root of all evil.
- God wants my happiness.

Eventually, when you don't draw a hard line on truth everything starts to blend together. For example, all things do work together for the good - "*...if you love Him and are called according to His purpose*" (Romans 8:28). It is not a blanket statement that everything in your life is going to work out. No one can guarantee when or if there's going to be healing, deliverance, or blessing.

I can say it's going to work out for your good if you love Him and are called according to His purpose, but His good might not be your goal. His good might not be what you call good. If you don't have a sure understanding and application of the Word of God, you're going to be susceptible to whatever the enemy brings your way and you may question what God says is good. (Especially when it doesn't feel good.)

If only we would take seriously the Word that God has already spoken to us. We don't need any new revelation or new information outside of the Bible. When we continue to study and take in the Word of God, He brings the right truth, at the right moment without fail.

Now we are prepared with our defensive armor and our offensive weapon, what do we do next? You may be surprised by Paul's instruction.

Stand firm.

Yep. That's it. Just stand there. Paul challenges us to put on the belt of truth, the breastplate of righteousness, the shoes that are the gospel of peace, the shield of faith, and the helmet of salvation. Then he tells us once we get everything on, we stand still. This may seem a little odd. It's definitely counterintuitive. It's our natural instinct to want to spring into action once we are prepared for battle but we are not called to pick fights with the devil. The Bible reminds repeatedly to be stable and stand firmly as believers. In 1 Corinthians 15:58 we are told to "be steadfast and immovable." Peter tells us to "*resist the devil*" and "*be firm in our faith* (I Peter 5:9)."

Praying at all times...

In order to stay watchful, wise, and discerning - we must pray. Prayer is not an optional activity nor is it reserved for laying a wish list before God. Prayer is the method by which we communicate with God. While the armor of God is the spiritual preparation for battle, prayer gives us the spiritual perspective.

Without prayer, we are soldiers without an understanding of our Commander's orders.

My friend, don't take lightly the need for prayer. We are desperate for direction from God. Once we are equipped, we need to be directed. And constantly so. This is not a one-time check-in, but a constant communication with God. Prayer is the gateway for discernment, wisdom, and ultimately victory.

Why do we need the armor of God?

Because we are at war and we must understand our adversary, put on our armor, and use our arsenal. If one thing is out of order, the enemy has a higher chance at success. We know what happens in our lives when our faith is shaky. When we're walking in unrighteousness, we're not even a threat. When we choose to believe lies and not truth or lay down the sword of the Spirit and not become familiar with the Word of God, we're ill-equipped to face our adversary. But once we are armored up, once we're prepared, there is no idea of defeat, depression, discouragement, or despair that the enemy can bring our way. The instructions are clear and initiative must be ours. Paul begins each phrase regarding the armor of God with an imperative - which is a verb or verb phrase that requires action. In essence, we are responsible for taking the initiative. We must "*put on* the full armor of God. *Gird ourselves* with truth. *Put on* the breastplate. *Put on* the gospel. *Take up* the shield. *Take* the helmet. *Pray* at all times." These are all imperatives. This is important because it gives us responsibility in getting ready. God lays out the armor but He's not going to get you dressed. Our God gives us the beauty of free will and choice. We must choose to be clothed in His armor and use His sword. God lets you choose Him for salvation. He didn't force it on you. Likewise, He lets you choose sanctification. The armor is at your feet. It's available and at your disposal. You can't let anybody tell you that you're incapable of knowing the Word, or you're incapable of radical faith, or consistent righteousness. It is possible. With the strength of God, you are capable — more importantly, you're called.

Is there a piece of armor you've put down? Are you effectively using your weapon of God's word?

Maybe there's a piece of armor you need to reacquaint yourself with. Do it today.

As the Lord moves, so does the enemy, so be prepared. He is not pleased that you're learning how to do battle. He would prefer that you resort to the old things that you've always been doing. But when you take seriously what God is doing, know that the enemy is coming your way. You must put on the armor of God and prepare to combat your adversary in a way that glorifies God and that will spread His Kingdom on this earth.

FOUR
PREVENTING FOOTHOLDS

For the weapons of our warfare are not of the flesh but have divine power to destroy strongholds.
2 Corinthians 10:4 (ESV)

What does it really mean to take thoughts captive?

When something is held captive that means it's bound; it's no longer free; it's under the rule and mastery of another. It's consumed by something; it is held captive by a particular thing. My hope is that by now you're realizing you have the ability to take every thought in your mind captive. Be aware of your adversary but understand he can be resisted. Put on your armor. Use your arsenal. You, my friend, are ready for war.

Let's look at the opening Scripture above. Underline or circle the word "strongholds." What is a stronghold? A *stronghold* is a term used in war meaning, a protected place where members of a military group stay and can defend themselves against attacks. If you want to defeat a city or nation, you attack the stronghold.

It's the military heart of a certain geographic area. It is usually a place surrounded by various types of protection – both natural (mountains, terrain, etc.) and man made (walls, bunkers, artillery, etc.). In this context, a spiritual stronghold is a commitment. It is a reinforced, faulty way of thinking based on a lie, and it governs and affects our thinking.

This battle of the mind goes beyond the power of positive thinking, mind control, good energy, or healthy environments because all those things are external. If we want to destroy strongholds we have to start by preventing footholds.

Note how strongholds are established. They start with a thought – a consideration; then you draw a conclusion or take a position on the matter. If you stick to this way of thinking, you move from a conclusion to a commitment and here is where our stronghold is built.

We mentally move from considerations to conclusions to commitments. In essence an idea becomes a belief and a belief becomes a lifestyle. The goal is to keep those false beliefs from taking root in the first place - when they are footholds. What does it mean to prevent footholds?

First we need to understand what is a foothold. Imagine receiving an unexpected knock on your door one evening. Without thinking you open the door. On the other side is somebody trying to break into your house. He steps his foot inside the door but you catch the door and begin to struggle to close it. The robber has one foot in the door - *a foothold.* He wants to come in and take over and establish a stronghold but you're trying to prevent that. This is the idea behind preventing footholds. Learning how to prevent footholds is the first step toward stopping a certain line of reasoning and this is where we want to take our thoughts captive. As soon as the lie gets a foot in the door of our minds we have to take it captive. We have to hold it hostage to the truth of God. Many of us skip over thoughts we should take captive, and when we allow those thoughts to sit there as footholds, they then become speculations and all of a sudden our life is being guided by a certain way of thinking.

The Old Testament story about the Tower of Babel gives us a great example. In Genesis, chapter 11, we find the story of people who decided they wanted to make a great name for themselves and build a tower to reach into heaven. Talk about lofty ideas. The hearts of the people were against God and they allowed prideful thoughts to run amuck instead of taking them captive. God ended up creating a language barrier among the people that prevented the tower from being built. Although God addressed it before it got too far, the real problem started before a brick was ever laid. It started as unchecked thoughts of discontentment, greed, and pride in the minds of individuals. Then when they came together and found agreement and consensus, a foothold was established. Our primary passage in 2 Corinthians 10 makes it clear that our unchecked thoughts can erect spiritual towers in our minds that compete against the knowledge of God. Look at verse 5:

> We destroy arguments and every lofty opinion raised against the knowledge of God, and take every thought captive to obey Christ,... (ESV)

When Paul refers to "lofty opinions raised against the knowledge of God," he's referring to situations like the Tower of Babel. We, in all of our humanity, determine we have better ideas than God and we choose to elevate, or raise, our opinions over God's truth.

The people in this story tried to physically elevate their thoughts over the knowledge of God. Today we often do the same thing in our spiritual and emotional decisions.

How do we resist? By taking every thought captive. Before the robber gets his foot in the door, we should know enough to not open the door in the first place. The first goal is prevention. We need to lock down the first wayward thought and keep it from entering the mental homes of our minds. The idea of taking every thought captive really means to take it prisoner. This is a habitual practice, a constant occurrence. It must be done every day. Don't give yourself credit for a "good" day. That's dangerous. Do you get proud of yourself when you do something holy? Don't get too distracted congratulating yourself. It's easy to get stuck when we have good moments but dwelling on a spiritual success makes us susceptible in other areas. There is no immunity for the believer. We are just as vulnerable ten years into our relationship with Christ as we are when we first begin. We must constantly scrutinize and imprison our thoughts so we can subject them to the obedience of Christ. We have to do that because Romans 7:23 says,

> "but I see a different law in the members of my body, waging war against the law of my mind and making me a prisoner of the law of sin which is in my members." (NASB)

Paul is talking about this internal conflict and he realizes if he doesn't make the first move towards taking his thoughts captive then his body's (flesh) going to take him captive. The same is true for us. We'll eventually become a prisoner to something, so we need to make sure we're prisoners to the cause of Christ. There is no neutral ground in spiritual warfare. You're either gaining ground or you're losing ground. Either you're going to take your thoughts captive to the obedience of Christ, or your body is going to take you captive and you're going to be under the law of sin. You're going to be subject to sin: a sinful lifestyle, a sinful pattern, sinful thinking. You have to take your thoughts captive when they form, and in whatever form they take. It can be just a quick idea, a consideration, the very first inkling when something pops into your mind and you immediately know, think, and/or say, "This is not right."

It's about preventing the progression.

To prevent footholds, we have to view the first thought as though it has already become a stronghold.

There's power in recognizing evil that first moment when a consideration enters your mind. We sometimes act as though we don't see it; but the truth is, when we get far enough down the road into whatever bad decision we've made, we can always look back on the first time we took a wrong turn. It just didn't seem that bad when the thought first entered your mind and neither did the decision you made. You can probably recall some purchases, relationships, and jobs you should have said "no" to. We often ignore the early warning signs when we are led by the flesh. To prevent footholds, we have to view the first thought as though it has already become a stronghold. We must treat it as though we already know where this thing was going to take us.

Have you ever ended a relationship that was really painful and run into the "ex" later in life? You may have seen that person and thought, *Hallelujah! Thank God I was saved from that!* Now when the relationship initially ended, it may not have felt like a *hallelujah moment.* Even though the person was toxic for you, it still hurt you because you just wanted to pray for God to fix the relationship and all of its cracks. But in His infinite wisdom and love He made it clear that He was not going to come to rescue a relationship that you had no business being in. As time passes and your heart is healed, the gratitude toward God is all that remains. Even though those experiences grow us up in Christ and give us grateful hearts, we can also work to keep it from getting that far. It's a progression; we don't fall in the moment, we fall step by step. The enemy, especially when you think you're "*mature,*" is not going to bring you to the end of the road and expect you to jump in the fire pit. He will just provide enticing things that draw you down a certain path and you won't even realize you're heading towards a dangerous end.

Psalm 1:1 gives an example of this progression.

> "Blessed is the man who does not walk in the counsel of the wicked, or stand in the way of sinners, or sit in the seat of scoffers." (ESV)

We see this progression displayed in our life decisions. When it comes to believing lies, it looks like this:

STEP 1: We start walking - heeding bad counseling.

STEP 2: We linger and "stand" there - we get stuck with bad company. We contemplate it and often end up making bad choices.

STEP 3: We finally take a seat and commit to a sinful way of life.

James 1:15 reads:

> "Then when lust has conceived, it gives birth to sin; and when sin is accomplished, it brings forth death." (NASB)

Throughout the Bible, we learn we don't just stumble into the deep pit of sin. A progression happens and we can use that same progression to subject our thoughts to the obedience of Christ. Our thoughts do not have to lead us into a sin trap. They can lead us to freedom. First, we have to take every single thought captive. Then, we have to prevent footholds, and ultimately, demolish, and tear down every stronghold.

Instead of falling into despair about your thought life, take action. Destroy those footholds (speculations). Just because you start to contemplate, and you consider a wrong way of thinking, the first time you act on it is really a speculation. It's like testing out the flawed way of thinking. If you continue on that path, you'll go from a consideration to a conclusion and adopt the sinful thinking as a part of your lifestyle.

Do you realize every time you choose your own course of action, instead of God's truth, you are declaring yourself supreme? And when you're supreme, you are your own god. When you are your own god, guess who you worship? You got it. You. That may sound extreme but it's true.

We can't have ideas, beliefs, or lifestyles that we have raised above what the Bible says to be true, and still come into the church and lift our hands declaring God is all we need or is Lord of all. Because in that moment, when *our* thinking reigns over our mind, God is <u>not</u> all we need, nor is He Lord of all. We become the answer for our own needs and we wear the crown of Lord over our own lives.

As a teenager, I challenged my parents' authority quite a few times. (Surprising right? I know.) You may recall this from your teenage years or it may be a reoccurring experience as you raise your own teenagers. But the truth is, teenagers think they know it all. They tend to challenge authority - teachers, parents, coaches, etc. As they grow in knowledge and learn about the world and life, they start to believe their knowledge is better than the knowledge of those who are responsible for them. You know whose knowledge they value based on whose truth they embrace. For example, my mom and dad told me 10:00 PM was my curfew on school nights. I, of course, thought midnight was a much better choice. So I stuck to the 10:00 PM curfew for a while but eventually, my own thinking got the best of me. On that fateful night, I didn't even stay out until midnight but I came home after 10:00 PM. My choice, demonstrated by my behavior, sent a message to my parents conveying my declaration of authority over them. My decision, in that moment, spoke volumes. I declared myself a better parent and the final authority in my life. I would be reminded later this was an invalid declaration. This is the same way we act with God. He says one thing, we think another, and the rebellion of building strongholds begins.

What are some of the common areas where we are susceptible to footholds?

- Unforgiveness/Anger/Entitlement
- Fear
- Doubt/Insecurity
- Discontentment
- Pride
- Disunity/Divisiveness
- Lust/Sexual Sin

The list can really go on and on. We know we have issues. We know our thoughts can get us in trouble. The real question of this chapter is: what do we do about that?

There are three choices I want to challenge you to make. They are simple in concept but spiritually challenging.

The first choice is:

starve it

If we want to begin to change our thinking, we have to deprive our minds of negative thoughts, temptations, and entrapments that are always lying before us. As we mentioned from Psalm 1:1, we have to remove bad council, remove bad company, and remove bad choices. Romans 13:14 says this: "*Put on the Lord Jesus Christ, and make no provision for the flesh in regard to its lust.*" If you know you're not supposed to have sugar, don't keep a cabinet full of cookies at home and tell yourself you're just going to be strong.(Look, I've tried it and it rarely works.)

We convince ourselves that moderation is a good substitute for elimination. Not true, my friends. Are you in (or have you been in) a relationship that needs to end? My advice – end it. Don't try to just be friends. Don't invite him or her to church in the name of godly love. Just end it. Are you on a strict financial mission to get out of debt and become the giver God created you to be? My advice – don't go window shopping. Don't try on things

We convince ourselves that moderation is a good substitute for elimination.

you might like. Don't try to figure out how this one item is "the exception." Don't even hang around your shopping friends unless they support your goals. Don't dangle anything tempting for the flesh to grab. We're human so we are going to fail, but we don't have to invite failure.

This also means we have to be cautious about things to which we expose ourselves. It's not just the thoughts that originate from within. It's the music we listen to, the TV shows and videos we watch, the movies we see, and the books we read. If you don't starve your mind of certain outside influences, those influences will affect your thinking. Have you ever noticed how the first time you watch or listen to something that blatantly contradicts your beliefs you are truly shocked? It takes a moment to even process what you're seeing or hearing. Then it takes several more moments to "get over it" and chalk it up to "the world we live in." It may even spur discussion with others as you inquire, "Did you see that?" or, "Can you believe this?" The Holy Spirit in us is unapologetically opposed to input that goes against God's standards and if we're listening, He will convict us and make us very uncomfortable.

Now, the second time your reaction may be a little different. Maybe you just roll your eyes, changes the channel or station and keep moving. You're resigned to the mess that is our society. By the third or fourth exposure you may not even notice. Or you may think to yourself, "They talk like that all the time. I don't talk like that. That's just how *they* talk." Suddenly you find yourself understanding why a married person wants to have an affair or worse – secretly rooting for the extramarital relationship to succeed. Great show writing, emotional and well-crafted lyrics, and plain old overexposure can numb us to the negative and unbiblical thoughts infiltrating our minds. If we want to begin to take thoughts captive, we have to starve our minds so we can cut the progression off before it begins.

saturate it

The second choice you must make in order to prevent footholds is to saturate your mind with truth. After you begin to develop a habit of starving your mind of things that carry even a hint of a lie, it's time to move on to the next step. You have to immerse or saturate your mind with the things that are true. Think back to Psalm 1. In verse 1, we are warned not to walk in bad council, choose bad company, or make bad choices. In verse 2 we are given the solution – delight in the law. This is not just a casual or crisis-driven action. The writer challenges us to "*meditate on it day and night.*" He wants us to feast on a diet of truth around the clock. Just as eating regularly protects us from malnourishment, taking in God's truth on a regular basis protects us from spiritual starvation. We are better prepared to use our spiritual armor to fight off imposters of truth when we stay rooted in what God has to say. And when we're rooted in God, it's nearly impossible for lies to take hold.

What does it look like to saturate your mind? Committing Scripture to memory, regular communication with God [prayer], and spending time with people who will spiritually sharpen you are all good habits. Even good worship music is a way to keep your mind on God. It's similar to the concept of allowing hot tea to steep. I'm a year-round hot tea drinker and I like my tea strong. In order to properly steep tea, you need to cover it. After you've poured your hot water over your tea bag (or leaves) you cover it for the desired amount of time.

You steep tea in order to infuse water into the dried tea leaves. This happens best when the water is hot. If you don't cover it, too much of the water is lost through evaporation or steam. So the cover keeps the hot water inside and brings dry tea leaves to life with moisture.

We want God's truth, brought to light by God's Spirit, to permeate every part of our minds.

But the Bible uses water as a metaphor for God's truth (Ephesians 5:26) and Jesus calls the Holy Spirit the Living Water (John 4:10 and 7:38). This is the water we want to be steeped in. We want God's truth, brought to light by God's Spirit, to permeate every part of our minds.

In tempting situations, God's truth reveals, in 1 Corinthians 10:13:

> "No temptation has overtaken you but such as is common to man; and God is faithful, who will not allow you to be tempted beyond what you are able, but with every temptation will provide a way of escape ,..." (NASB)

When things and people around you seem to make it hard to find peace, know you have this gift from Jesus, "*Peace I leave with you; My peace I give to you; not as the world gives do I give to you. Do not let your heart be troubled, nor let it be fearful.*" (John 14:27 NASB). And when negativity, lies, shame, guilt, insecurity, etc. try to worm their way into your head, remember, "*...whatever is true, whatever is honorable, whatever is right, whatever is pure, whatever is lovely, what-ever is of good* *repute, if there is any excellence and if anything worthy of praise, dwell on these things."* (Philippians 4:8 NASB)

share it

The third choice we need to make is to share our journey. The enemy loves isolation. He wants you to think if you try hard enough you can do it by yourself. He will try to convince you that nobody else is going through what you're going through or that they won't understand. So many reasons of rationalization creep into our minds to keep us isolated. Proverbs 28:13 provides this wisdom: *"He who conceals his transgressions will not prosper, but he who confesses and forsakes them will find compassion."* And James 5:16 instructs, *"...confess your sins to one another, and pray for one another so that you may be healed."* (NASB) Not only should we confess to God, we should confess to each other. When we choose transparency in healthy communities of faith, we can find freedom from footholds. We have to resist the temptation to try to fix ourselves in private but instead foster healthy, growing spiritual connections with people who will challenge us and grow with us.

I have always loved watching makeover shows. The topic could be dramatic weight loss, drastic re-design of a home, or helping someone find personal style. The goal of these shows is to give you an idea of the "before." They want you to understand the starting condition of whatever/whomever is being made over. You go on a journey with the subject of the show. At the end of the show there's a big reveal. It's always amazing to see the transformation. However, the impact of the "after" depends heavily on how well the "before" was documented. The better the audience understands the severity and desperation of a situation, the more impactful the transformation. This understanding is achieved through transparency. The subjects of the show have to be willing to share the raw truth about their scenario in order for the audience to appreciate the final outcome. This is the spirit behind sharing in community. The aim is to invite people on the journey with you, not just show off your medal at the finish line. Just like any distance race, you will need supporters along the way. The Christian race is a marathon not a sprint.

As you're processing this, the idea of accountability may come to mind. For decades accountability relationships have been touted as solutions to sinful lifestyles. I will agree they are important; however, accountability is not the same as living in authentic community. It's certainly a part of it, but it's only one aspect. Accountability simply means the ability to give an account of something; to give a report so to speak. I can be accountable to you and tell you what's going on in my life and still keep our relationship very shallow. That's different from inviting you to witness what's going on in my life, good or bad. It's a contrast from intentionally integrating you into my life so that we journey together. Authentic community is built around both the mundane and major activities of life. Community can be fostered from working together, sharing birthdays and dinners, arranging playdates with the kids, going through a book together, discussing the latest sermon or Bible study series and, of course, being present in times of crisis. In these happenings of life, we learn about each other, build trust, and earn the right to speak truth to one another. We can begin to pick up on one another's unhealthy thinking when we spend time together. It's what I call "doing life together." We need to do more than report spiritual or sin activity. We need to intentionally share in spiritually healthy communities. What I'm really saying is if you want to prevent footholds - it takes a village.

Dear friend, I urge you to take seriously this effort in preventing footholds. Don't let considerations turn into speculations and ultimately into strongholds.

I implore you to make these three wise choices:

1. STARVE your mind of what is unhealthy and what is ungodly. Be wise about the various inputs of information to which you are exposed.
2. SATURATE your mind with things to align with the truth of God.
3. SHARE your life with a community of Christians who can give you conviction, compassion, and consistently.

FIVE
DESTROYING STRONGHOLDS

This is where the progression, unchecked, ends. When footholds aren't prevented but allowed to take root and produce bad thinking, you find yourself fighting the strongholds in your mind.

Remember in the beginning of our journey together when I shared some experiences I'd had with believers struggling with strongholds? In each of those stories, a thought was planted in their minds that wasn't uprooted. Over time, that thought grew deep roots and began to bear its own kind of fruit. My friends didn't go from joy in the Lord on Monday to suicidal thoughts on Tuesday. They didn't have a healthy marriage one day and a destructive one the next. The progression is real. You may now be thinking of some footholds in your own life that have gone untouched. Maybe God has brought a stronghold to your mind or opened your eyes to see a deep struggle that you need to address. While the goal is prevention, we can still destroy strongholds with our *divine weapons* of spiritual warfare. Regardless of where we are in the progression of unchecked thoughts, there's hope. Not wishful thinking, or fingers-crossed type of hope. There is guaranteed hope that's rooted in heaven and gives us power here on earth (Colossians 1:5).

So what does Paul mean when he says we can destroy strongholds? A stronghold is a military word that indicates the centralized place or strongest point of a city or region. If an enemy were to attack, they would target the stronghold. That is where all the great thinking of that city's culture would rest. It is almost like a modern city hall. If the enemy wipes out the centralized place of the city, then he has the whole city. In a spiritual context, a stronghold is the central hub of sin. It is a powerful presence in our lives.

I believe Paul uses this imagery so we can understand the seriousness and strength of any thinking that goes against the truth of the Bible. He wants us to understand that when we get to this point, we are actually under the guidance of the faulty thinking rather than our heavenly Father! This kind of bondage parallels the strength of a fortified city, or fortress (another word for stronghold), and it will take intentional spiritual work to tear it down. This is no small or trivial thing. When mental strongholds exists in our minds, they become our new truth; and that's a very dangerous reality.

Strongholds have multiple sources and can appear in different forms. The most common include psychological and religious strongholds.

Psychological strongholds are practiced, habitual ways of thinking, and they often can lead to addictive, negative habits and lifestyles. Psychological strongholds can fill you with anxiety, stress, and hopelessness, and they will convince you that a situation can never change or that life is going to always look the same.

Psychological strongholds can negatively impact the body too. For example, you may struggle with envy or discontentment. Maybe you gripe more than you're grateful or you have a hard time rejoicing with others. Envy may be a stronghold for you. Look at Proverbs 14:30. It says, "*A heart at peace gives life to the body, but envy rots the bones.*" (NASB) Envy is juxtaposed to peace in this verse. It does more than make you sad or give you a hard day. The writer of this proverb wants you to know envy can be something so entrenched in our minds that most of our decisions and direction are driven by discontentment. That discontentment can destroy our bodies over time. You, or someone you know, may wrestle with depression and/or anxiety. Medical professionals will testify how often anxiety attacks or panic attacks are confused for heart attacks and vice versa. If you've ever struggled with an addiction or known someone who struggles with addiction, you will understand how severely our thinking can impact us physically. Even if you believe depression, anxiety, etc. are genetic or biological, you should also accept that our psyche – our minds – can significantly impact our biology.

Demonic strongholds are another kind of stronghold we face in this spiritual battle. The good news is, as believers, we cannot be possessed by a demon. We cannot be under the control of a demon, however, we can definitely be influenced by a demon. Demonic strongholds start with our thoughts and that's where they must be dealt with.

If we go back to Matthew 16, to the exchange between Peter and Jesus, Peter thought he was doing something upstanding and noble. He was passionately defensive of Jesus when he spoke against the unpleasant future Jesus was revealing. When Peter said, "*Lord, may it never be.*" Jesus didn't respond with gratitude for Peter's passion. Instead, Jesus said, "*Get behind Me, Satan.*" It's not that Jesus didn't feel Peter did not have real affection for Him. Jesus' response was so passionate because He was clearly sharing the will (or truth) of God and Peter, in his limited knowledge, thought he knew better.

In that instance, it would seem like Peter had good intentions and would probably have said, "Lord, You didn't have to call me Satan. That's kind of harsh. I meant well." But Jesus didn't care about Peter's intentions. Any time you elevate your thoughts against what God has already said, you're under the influence of Satan. When Peter heard that information from Jesus, he didn't say, "Satan, what do you think about that?" There was a thought in Peter's mind that said, *No, I love the Lord, and we need Him here. That cannot be the best plan. I don't think what Jesus is saying is the best way to go.* In that moment, he had a thought that elevated itself over the knowledge of Jesus Christ, over the knowledge of the will of God, and in that moment, Jesus identified him with Satan, the father of lies.

That is exactly what happens to us when we have demonic strongholds. You might not be frothing at the mouth with your head spinning, but this is what happens. Even with good intentions, it is easy to walk down a path that elevates our own knowledge against the knowledge of God.

Religious strongholds show up as in our minds as false teaching and false doctrine. I'm not talking about us gathering in places where people are preaching with snakes and trying to do things that are obviously extreme. The more you grow in Christ and the wiser and more mature you become as a believer, the more strategic the enemy will become when he comes for you.

When you start to believe ideas such as, *God's grace is conditional* or *salvation isn't secure*, it can drastically alter your relationship with God and with others. You start to interpret every closed door, unpleasant circumstance, and hardship as a result of something you've done wrong. Which in turn, creates a strain on your relationship with God as you try to fix your behavior in order to guide His hand or negotiate your needs with Him rather than see everything He does as an expression of love.

False teachings can lead us to believe that our circumstances, not just our consequences, come from sin. When you believe that the Lord gives you certain circumstances because of sin, you will fall into the same good works pattern that is the struggle of many Christ followers.

False doctrine and false teaching can creep up on us. When you want to challenge false doctrine and false teaching, ask yourself if your beliefs are confirmed and affirmed in the Word of God. False teaching is easily perpetuated when we are unfamiliar with the sword of the Spirit or don't take up the belt of truth. These pieces of our armor inform our minds as to what is true according to God.

In short, strongholds originate in the mind, and they can be sexual, financial, relational, and many other types. Trauma from our past, the influence of our parents, and our life experiences can be gateways to destructive thinking. But regardless of the origin, you still have a choice in how you respond. Even though the enemy cannot build the stronghold in your mind, he can hand you the bricks, and you get to decide whether or not you're going to take them.

That is empowering. You can't put all the blame on the enemy because it's not his fault where you allow your thoughts and your behavior to go. In the same way God granted us free will to choose Him for salvation, we have free will over the enemy. When you embrace this, you can destroy things you may have subconsciously built in your mind. This power that we have from God removes the excuses of helplessness. There are times when it's easier to be helpless victims and targets of the enemy so we don't have to own our thinking and our choices. The Bible says you are empowered to take thoughts captive. You have the weapons to destroy strongholds.

Stay vigilant so you won't be vulnerable to the plans of your adversary.

Destroying strongholds is not for the faint of heart. It's a long journey that demands consistent effort. Like a recovering drug addict or alcoholic, you must remain committed to uprooting unhealthy and untrue thoughts. You never reach a point where you let your guard down. Stay vigilant so you won't be vulnerable to the plans of your adversary. This is not a cosmetic touch up but spiritual surgery. And like any other surgery, you must submit to the hand of the surgeon in order for it to be successful. Nothing can deliver you from strongholds if you don't choose to submit to the Spirit of God. Your pastor cannot take your thoughts captive. The one who has the gift of prayer cannot take your thoughts captive. A gathering where Christians get together and talk about why they're hurting cannot take your thoughts captive. Only you—the same one who chose salvation, the same one who chose sanctification, the same one who chose to die with Christ and be resurrected with Christ—can take your thoughts captive.

In order to subject our strongholds to spiritual surgery, there are two things we need to resist.

First, we have to resist the urge to band-aid our brokenness. It is tempting to succumb to band-aid remedies, where we tell ourselves, one good worship song or one good cry will fix us. Sometimes we claim that a day off, spa treatment or a good night's sleep with do the trick. Other times we go with deeper remedies of chocolate or ice cream (or both).

You have to resist the temptation to band-aid the brokenness because the goal is not better behavior; the goal is mastery of the mind. If your goal is only better behavior, you'll start to give yourself credit because you're acting right for a few minutes, but your heart hasn't changed. Jesus told the Pharisees in Matthew 23:27-28, "*...you are like whitewashed tombs, which look beautiful on the outside but on the inside are full of the bones of the dead and everything unclean. In the same way, on the outside you appear to people as righteous but on the inside you are full of hypocrisy and wickedness*" (NASB).

My husband and I have a three year-old son, and we really emphasize the importance of good manners with him. I'm always encouraging him to speak to those who speak to him and make eye contact while doing so. I constantly remind him to say "Thank you," "Please," and to address adults with "Ms." or "Mr." At three years old, he doesn't know why he's doing it, but we're trying to instill this within him as normal behavior, so as he gets older, he'll see these things as signs of respect, humility, and gratitude.

Because he's young and immature, the focus on behavior can work for now. As he grows older, if I never explain my thinking, his behavior will probably fade. He's going to reach a certain age and he may think these behaviors are unnecessary. He will decide if he wants to continue acting that way. Without understanding the principle behind the behavior he will probably choose the behavior he thinks is right. He could make a good choice but he could make a selfish choice too. Our job is to make sure he understands the reason behind these actions so they have meaning to him.

We are not addressing the action. We are addressing our hearts, so we can affect our thoughts.

Secondly, you have to resist the temptation to strategize your stronghold. It's tempting to say, "This thing has taken over; it's getting out of control. I need to figure out a way to beat this thing. If I can just sit down and think about it, I probably can figure out a strategy because that's how I've solved every other problem in life."

It doesn't matter how smart or strategic you are, you have to start from the inside out. It's a deep, and sometimes painful, process to constantly arrest the thoughts that cross our minds but it's the only way to have lasting change.

With these two warnings in mind, there are three efforts you need to embrace if you want to tear down your strongholds. Armies who successfully defeat their enemies have excellently executed these three efforts. They have 1) examined the target to understand the best way to attack, 2) exposed the target to the soldiers that will help bring it down, and once the target was defeated, 3) established the new authority.

5.1

EXAMINE THE HEART

Search me, O God, and know my heart; test me and know my anxious thoughts. Psalm 139:23 (NASB)

The first thing we must do is regularly examine our hearts. The Scripture above is the cry of David inviting God to look closely at his heart. It's not that God doesn't already know our thoughts; but when we submit to regular examination by inviting the Divine Examiner, He can show us things we might not see with our limited, human perspective.

According to Jeremiah 17:9 "*The heart is more deceitful than all else and is desperately sick: who can understand it?*" In the next verse (10) the Lord responds and says, "*I, the Lord, search the heart, I test the mind, even to give to each man according to his ways, according to the results of his deeds.*" (NASB)

We learn from Jeremiah 17 we're setting ourselves up to fail when we rely on our emotions, intuition, and feelings. The heart is deceitful, and that is why we have to subject ourselves to regular examination. As we get more and more savvy, our thought life will become increasingly difficult to manage. Our wayward thoughts will take more subtle forms. If we aren't constantly assessing them or measuring them against God's truth, it may be weeks, months, or years before we realize something is wrong. Hebrews 4:12 tells us, "*The word of God is living and active, and sharper than any two-edged sword, and is able to divide soul and spirit, joints and marrow, discerning the thoughts and the intentions of the heart*" (NASB).

We need to go to the Word, not just for comfort, but for conviction.

We need to go to the Word, not just for comfort, but for conviction. Every time I read God's Word I experience conviction. I walk away challenged in so many areas. Whether it's how I submit (or not) to my husband, if I conveyed my thoughts with love to the people I encountered on a particular day, or even how well I'm caring for my temple with healthy eating, exercise, and rest. Even when reading the Psalms or passages of Scripture that encourage and give hope, I am reminded of how undeserving I am. I am grateful that God's goodness is not based on my goodness. The Word of God can get in my soul and do surgery like nothing, or no one else can. If you would submit yourself to regular examination, there is no way you can constantly stay in the Word of God and not get convicted. Regular examination allows us to survey our minds for thoughts that need to be taken captive whether they're just forming or have already become strongholds.

To hear the conviction of the Holy Spirit clearly, we have to pray and ask God to remove our preconceived notions and self-centered needs when we come to His Word.

When I go to see my doctor, I often provided suggestions regarding my health. (I'm sure he loves this.) We are in the age of accessible and abundant information. With just a little bit of searching, I can find what I'm looking for online. I can find a website where I simply enter my symptoms and it gives a suggested diagnosis. So I take these suggestions to my doctor in order to help him help me. Isn't that thoughtful of me? I thought so too. He did not. He usually responds by reminding me many symptoms are not visible to the eye and even if they were, various combinations of symptoms can be driven by different root causes. Each body is different so it's his job to do a more thorough assessment to understand the problem and the prognosis. In his very nice way he's telling me to let him do what he's been trained to do. My job is to come to him, willing to receive his knowledge, and ready to take action based on that knowledge.

This same approach works with God's Word. We can't come to Him with suggestions for the solution to our situation. We are supposed to come willing to receive His knowledge, even if we don't like it, and be ready to take actions based on that knowledge. That is the definition of wisdom.

There are some questions that we need to begin thinking about when we submit our hearts to regular examination.

QUESTION 1:
Am I inviting the Surgeon (God) to examine me?

Are you like me bringing your symptoms and suggested diagnosis to God? Trust me, He doesn't need your help. We must go to God willing to submit ourselves to His thorough examination.

QUESTION 2:
How do I respond when His truth cuts and convicts me?

Being exposed to and having a steady diet of the Word is one thing. It's important that we do that, but the questions we ask

We need to apply knowledge and truth, not simply acquire it.

ourselves and the time spent in reflection are just as important. We need to apply knowledge and truth, not simply acquire it. This journey is about quality, not quantity. You don't have to read the Bible in a year. You can take one verse, and "chew" on it slowly and thoughtfully.

QUESTION 3:
Do I have any negative images of God?

On this mission, we will also have to assess what we think about God. What you believe about God is the single most defining thought you have as a follower of Christ. These negative images of God usually come from our past experiences, flawed theology, and/or our relationship, or lack thereof, with our earthly father. If you experience trauma during your childhood you may see God as distant or a selective protector. You may feel He failed you. If you have suffered consequences from your own bad decisions you might view God as angry or unforgiving. Maybe you were taught that God's love equates to prosperity, health, and minimal trouble in life. If that's the case, you will see every illness, financial struggle, or family hardship as God's disapproval when it may in fact simply be His divine sovereignty.

QUESTION 4:
How do I respond to my view of God?

This of course builds on the previous question. Not only do you need to be aware of how you see God but you must be mindful of how your opinion of God impacts your decisions and choices.

Let me give you a few examples of how this can become important in tearing down strongholds. If you think God is angry, you will live a life characterized by fear. You'll think that every time you do something wrong, you're going to be "in trouble" with God because all you've seen of God is what you perceive to be His anger. Believing God is unforgiving leads to consciously or unconsciously trying to earn His forgiveness. You'll feel like you're perpetually in trouble. That's the equivalent of walking on spiritual egg shells. It negates the gifts of freedom and grace for the believer. It will affect how you hear from God and it will color the lens through which you see Scripture and receive truth.

It could even cause you to live like you're not good enough, so life is spent trying to earn God's favor. You want God to be pleased but you're doing it not from the inside out, but from the outside in because you think He's always mad at you, and if you don't do right, you're going to be in trouble. Maybe you had a parent who expressed loved toward you based on success or achievement. It's easy to transfer that philosophy to your relationship with God. If you believe you have to earn God's approval or acceptance, you might be the person who's going to climb every corporate ladder. Achievement is the end goal. You make a vow to yourself to never be at the bottom or to avoid status quo and mediocrity. Those goals can be great if they are rooted in truth. However, if you're striving for excellence in hope of God's acceptance, it may lead to choices that belittle others, push ethical boundaries, feed greed, etc. A stronghold of greed or achievement may be lurking in your mind, influencing your thoughts about God. Instead, you should strive for excellent *from* a place of acceptance not *for* acceptance. You're already accepted by God, your excellence should reflect His glory not merely your personal goals.

I wish we could simply decide to do better, forget the past and start with a clean slate of new thinking. In reality, we need to look backward before we can move forward.

If you have the mindset that God does not want to be near you, you'll struggle when people talk about intimacy with God. You'll struggle when people say they hear the Lord or felt His presence and comfort. If you're that person, you'll be wondering what they're talking about or questioning why you've never experienced it. If you have a hard time visualizing God as an intimate Father, someone who wants a close connection with you, someone who's not aloof and distant, then guess what? You're going to struggle with isolation. You're going to have a hard time connecting with other people if you don't feel connected to God. Even if you don't physically isolate yourself, you can emotionally isolate yourself from others. You may choose to minimize conflict with emotional distance but you'll also eliminate authentic community. When things go wrong, you will request that others "give you your space." Words like "fine," "good," or "okay" become standard responses when you're asked about your well-being. You push the hurt and disappointment down a little further and maybe even become emotionally unavailable. This is the short-term way to guard your feelings when you are hurt. You can just pretend nothing bothers you because once you acknowledge that you're hurt or offended, or your emotions are even on the table, then you have to deal with them. If you can't understand God's desire to be intimate and close with you, you may have a stronghold that convinces you that you aren't worth the emotional work of an intimate relationship. That's when the truth that we are the imago dei (the image of God) can be transforming.

These are just a few ways that our thinking can become so

prominent in our life that we resort to defensive behavior patterns to avoid dealing with whatever hurts.

Regular examination is more than just having "quiet time." It is more than just making sure we get in our Scripture reading. A verse a day does not keep the devil away - the devil is good at quoting verses too. Quoting Scripture without being convicted by Scripture is inconsequential. It's about being convicted and convinced, and actually considering what the Word of God is saying. Examination is considering each truth about God and asking yourself if you believe it and if your life is living proof of it.

We need to stop and ask God, "What truth do I need to digest?" There are some hidden lies that most of us have expertly woven into our lives and we are not even aware they are there. You have to take a few moments every day, every week, and sit before God. Unhurried time with God is the foundation for the spiritual examination we constantly need.

QUESTION 5:
When did I first surrender to this lie?

Wait, what? Ok you may have been tracking with me until this point but now you might be wondering where I'm going with this question. Why on earth do we need to go digging up the past? Isn't it better to leave it where it belongs? You know, in the past! That may seem like the simple answer but without looking back and understanding some of the root causes of our issues, a solution to address them will not reach beyond the surface. It may not make sense now or sound exciting, but there is value in finding the source of our hurt and pain. It's important to understand the first time you took that detour in your thinking. Was it hurt caused to you? Were you on the receiving end of trauma? Were there lies you had been fed? Were you betrayed?

Many psychologists and therapists will agree with this theory but more importantly, it's in the Bible.

Look at Revelation 2:4-5 (NASB), Jesus is talking to the church at Ephesus, a group of believers who have lost their way. He says,

> "But I have this against you, that you have left your first love. Therefore remember from where you have fallen, and repent and do the deeds you did at first..."

The church at Ephesus had fallen out of love with Jesus. He realized that their relationship had become routine. It had become mundane. If you've ever been in a relationship like that, whether it's a marriage or just a dating relationship, you know it always starts on a high, but something happens along the way that causes it to fizzle or plateau. Usually, that moment of realization is not the point of the decline. If you retrace your steps, you can often look back and realize things have been declining for a while. Maybe you chose to ignore or band-aid it, but the signs of decline were there.

If you're trying to find the root of issues in a relationship you have to go back to that place where the hurt or detour first happened. That is exactly what Jesus is saying in this passage. He realizes this church is no longer prioritizing Him as their first love. To address this problem, He commands them to remember where it all went wrong. He knows that where they are today isn't the beginning of the problem. Jesus doesn't want them to simply correct their behavior, He wants them to look beneath the surface and that requires looking back. In regular examination, it's very important to take a look at where we first made that detour. That in and of itself is a process. We need to ask God to show us the beginning of the lies, hurt, shame, etc. and be prepared and patient on the journey knowing He's leading the way.

The process doesn't end when you arrive at the beginning. That won't be enough to alter your way of thinking. Look back at Revelation 2:4. Jesus says that after you remember, He wants you to repent.

Do you know what repent means? It means to change your mind. It means to change direction. Our prayer should be, "God, send me back there to where it first happened." WARNING: This might not be fun. You're probably not going to be clicking your heels together and having a victory celebration. It's not fun at all to invite God to walk you through some pain that you've spent a lot of time trying to bury but it is necessary if we desire to change beneath the surface.

I'll never forget the time I walked into the home of one my friends and was greeted by the blissful aroma of warm, sugary strawberries. I prayed earnestly as I made my way to the kitchen that what I was smelling was fresh strawberry cake and not one of those weird candles that smell like strawberry cake. (My apologies to those that like food-scented candles.) To my joy, as I entered the kitchen, a freshly-iced strawberry cake awaited me - I think I heard it whisper my name. I served myself a slice of cake, without invitation, because that's what real friends do – they self-invite. I sat down to savor what was sure to be an amazing experience. I slowly slid the fork through my slice and prepared my palette to be blessed by the first bite. The fresh strawberry icing hit my mouth and my eyes began to roll back in my head. The first taste of the cake followed and my eyes froze mid-roll. My forehead wrinkled in confusion as I tried to make sense of what I was tasting. Underneath that delicious icing was a substance that made me think I had accidentally bit into a Styrofoam cup. I looked at my fork. It *looked* like cake. It was the *color* of cake. But real cake would have been offended by this impostor. And because I'm just a nice person, I lovingly told my friend something was very wrong with my cake experience. She tasted the cake and realized I was not exaggerating. As she sat trying to recount what could have gone wrong, I did the most sympathetic thing I could think of. You guessed it. I proceeded to scrape of the icing and enjoy the best part of the cake. I gave my friend a fork too and we had a great time. It was really good icing.

My point is, we don't want our lives to be worthless beneath the surface. There are few things more disappointing than realizing the exterior of something or someone is the best part. The icing should be highlighting the cake – not hiding it. The outfit should draw you into the person - not define her. The curb appeal of a house doesn't replace the character of it. In the same way, if you don't walk back through that pain, all you're going to be doing is adding spiritual "icing" to a bad tasting "cake." When we talk about regular examination, it is important to figure out where we first surrendered to the lie, or where we first detoured from the truth. Jesus says you have to change your thinking about the original lie.

We often tell ourselves that we have a healthy image of God but our behavior doesn't line up with that healthy image. Our behavior usually tends to be skewed toward whatever we believe to be true about God. When we begin to destroy a stronghold, we don't want to assume that we can outsmart our strongholds or that we can band-aid the brokenness. We don't want to just sing more songs and read more Scripture and come to more Bible studies and think that somehow it's just going to work itself out. It's not just adding more righteousness on top of the sin. It has to be an intentional adding of righteousness and an intentional ridding of sin. We should keep our hearts and our thoughts open for examination. Our heart is deceitful and it's a mess. In Psalm 139, the psalmist reminds us that we have to cry out to God to search our hearts. We have to invite Him in to look at the mess and to help us be realistic and gain the proper perspective about what we're seeing.

When I'm regularly examining my heart, I'm opening myself up and I'm asking God to search me and know me. I have to go beyond the surface to deal with the mess. If I don't take it seriously and understand the nature of the work that has to be done, it's like having a heart attack and taking some Neosporin, and rubbing it on my chest. That sounds silly. It's not because Neosporin isn't good or because Neosporin doesn't work. Neosporin works for the right injury. But if I try to take something that's meant for a surface cut and apply it to an internal issue, I'm just going to end up with greasy skin.

As we start to unlock truth that has been hidden and embedded in our minds for so long, we'll be able to effectively use the tools we have been given to tear down strongholds. Go before God, let Him speak to you. You don't have to talk first. He will begin to show you things you didn't even realize were there.

5.2
EXPOSE THE LIES

Whoever conceals his transgressions will not prosper, but he who confesses and forsakes them will obtain mercy. Proverbs 28:13 (NASB)

Now it's time to embrace the next effort in tearing down strongholds. We must expose the darkness and lies that bind us - and we must do so relentlessly. The Bible says that the darkness does not like the light. You have to be relentless about — not randomly interested in - exposing the thoughts that have become the bricks of strongholds we've built in our minds.

One way I would encourage you to begin exposing your thinking to the Word of God is to just write down some of the flawed thinking that you know you're wrestling with. I would venture to say that there are many times when we have flawed thinking that's so deep we've not even figured it all out. When we pray, we can't even always verbalize our need. If you're like me, sometimes you just go to God confessing you're a mess. There may be so many unhealthy thoughts swirling around your head that you may feel overwhelmed. You might not know where to start. In those moments, simply ask God. Ask Him where He wants you to start. He won't overwhelm you. He'll give something you and He can tackle together.

The first step is to expose it (admit it) to yourself. Come face-to-face with that thought or lie by saying it out loud. That may sound a little scary. The good news is God already knows. You're not going to shock Him. (You know He's omniscient and all.)

My grandmother used to challenge me when I prayed to name my sins specifically. I liked to pray, "Lord, forgive me for my sins." She would say, "What sins?" I'd reply with, "I'm not telling you." (I mean, really?) She would tell me, "Jada, I'm going to leave this room, but you need to tell God what you did today." My response would be, "He already knows. You told me He knows everything." She would tell me, "He knows, but He wants to know that you know."

Whoa.

Exposure means being as precise about your sin as you are about your prayer requests.

Exposure means being as precise about your sin as you are about your prayer requests. When we need something from God we have a date, time, amount, location, etc. that we pray about. But when it comes to confession, a blanket request for forgiveness seems to satisfy us. It's one thing to ask God to forgive me for my sins. It's another thing to be specific. For example:

- God forgive me for acting in vanity and greed with the purchases I made today.
- God, forgive me for the intentionally hurtful words I said to my husband today.
- God, forgive me for walking the other way when I noticed my coworker may have needed and encouraging word or

listening ear.

- God forgive me for letting lust guide my actions today.

There is some value to exposing the darkness in your mind to yourself first, because often we are not being very honest with ourselves. We want to think that we're better than we are and God is waiting for us to begin to embrace truth. When you don't see yourself as you really are, you don't work on getting healthier because you think you are okay. More importantly, you can't understand your heavenly Father's love and grace for you because you don't fully embrace your need for it.

A few times on my personal journey, I was brought back to where I first fell out of love. There's nothing like getting to that place. You're crying, you're sad, and you're broken as you realize the mess that you are. The Holy Spirit is "rubbing your back" saying, "*I already knew, child, I already knew.*" That is what makes you lift your hands and worship—not a job promotion, not things going well—but being back in that place where you originally left your first love and realizing He never left you.

It is then you realize that at the bottom of your brokenness God was already standing there with arms open wide. He lavishes us with grace and mercy and the more we are aware of our need for it, the more we appreciate it. If you think you have it all together, you won't need any mercy, let alone God's mercy. If you brush over your sin and spend all your time on your request, then all you crave is the blessing and grace of God but you'll miss the mercy of God.

As an added benefit, a good healthy confession time will put all your prayer requests in perspective. Just spend enough time telling God how you've disappointed Him in a day and by the time you get to your requests your prayer will take on a different tone. Perspective changes everything. You will be praying, "God, whatever You think is best... I just realized I should be glad to be alive right now. Whatever You think is best. Amen."

There is nothing like good confession. Exposure is important because when we expose ourselves, we're exposing ourselves to God's truth, not our own truth. When we expose ourselves to the truth, the truth can and will convict us.

Let's look at Lamentations 2:14-15 (NASB). We find God upset with the children of Israel. He says, "*Your prophets have seen for you false and foolish visions; and they have not exposed your iniquity so as to restore you from captivity, but they have seen for you false and misleading oracles. All who pass along the way clap their hands in derision at you; they hiss and they shake their heads at the daughter of Jerusalem, 'Is this the city which they said, "the perfection of beauty, of joy to all the earth?" ' "*

We see from these two verses that the Lord, through the prophet Jeremiah, is admonishing the people for listening to lies from false prophets. The prophets painted a pleasing picture that was highly inaccurate. Instead of telling Israel the ugly truth and exposing their sin, they gave prophecies that made the people think they were doing better than they actually were. This may sound familiar. In many of our churches today, the main message is to make people feel good about life. We are hearing messages that tell us everything will be alright, things aren't as bad as they seem, and things will get better. The truth is sometimes painful but you need to cling to it. Do you remember the belt of truth from Ephesians 6:14? It's that same principle being demonstrated here. Secrets just fuel strongholds. As long as you keep God's truth hidden you will stay in bondage and have no chance to truly be free.

Jeremiah says the prophets of Israel preached "*false and foolish visions*" about God. In our key passage, 2 Corinthians 10, Paul calls it "*lofty knowledge raised up against that of God.*" The children of Israel tried to follow a knowledge they thought was higher than God's knowledge, and that is why they stayed in captivity.

God's truth might not draw hundreds of thousands - after all Jesus walked through many cities and sometimes drew only a small crowd. But God's truth will set you free and that's the goal of relentless exposure. It's about exposing your thoughts to yourself, to the Word of God, and ultimately to a trusted community. It goes against the notion of isolation and the desire to keep life hidden. Relentless exposure opposes the spirit of independence that we tend to embrace as we navigate life. It keeps us from being our only filter and invites others to speak God's truth into our lives. More importantly, it shows the world, and everyone watching, what it looks like to follow Jesus - flaws and all. Believing your own version of truth is not only about your own freedom; it's about the glory of God. When you minimize the truth of God and elevate your own truth, you reshape the image of God in the eyes of nonbelievers. You're telling nonbelievers you are not really comfortable with the real truth of God, so you need to create a more palatable version. That plan can backfire. Instead of drawing people to God with a glossy version of the truth, it can lead people to conclude they can create their own version of truth as well. Who needs absolute truth if we're making it up as we go? And who is God without His absolute truth?

Yes, this tailored truth is a dangerous path to play on.

Ephesians 5:11-13 (NASB) says, "*Do not participate in the unfruitful deeds of darkness, but instead expose them; for it is disgraceful even to speak of the things which are done by them in secret. But all things become visible when they are exposed to the light, for everything that become visible is light.*" Paul is dropping a load of knowledge right here. He tells us to be relentless about exposure. When you expose your thinking to other believers who are in safe community, then all that junk that's hiding in the darkness can begin to diminish because darkness does not like light. The word "light" there is the same word that Jesus uses in Matthew 5 where He commands, "*Let your light shine before men in such a way that they may see your good works,...*" and earlier in that same chapter where He informs, "*You are the light of the world.*"

We live in a world that is more connected than ever before but what good are those connections in the absence of community?

James 5:16 states, "*Therefore, confess your sins one to another,...* " (NASB) See that phrase, "one to another" in there? Yes, you guessed it. He's talking about community again. Confessing to ourselves and to God shouldn't be the end of our relentless exposure. We live in a world that is more connected than ever before but what good are those connections in the absence of community? Connections may be where you turn in times of celebration but they are not where you turn in times of crisis. In crisis, you need and want real community. People who have chosen to create a safe place for you to share your journey. Notice I said *safe* not *perfect*. Since community consists of people, I can guarantee it won't be perfect. They will fail. They will mess up sometimes, but we don't invite others into our lives solely to bring us comfort and encouragement. We invite them because transparency with others transforms *us*. We become more humble. We become more aware. Even when our community disappoints, it's to our benefit because it can draw us to be more dependent on God and more forgiving of others. It's a win-win situation.

Having made my sales pitch for community, I need to add that it's only as good as you make it. You have to be honest if you hope to gain any fruit from it. I recently met a woman who said her marriage was in crisis. She and her husband were on the verge of divorce. This couple has been in a community group for two years and no one in their group knew that they were reaching the breaking point in their marriage. Why is that? Because every time the members of the group asked them how they were doing, they said they were fine. Now they are in crisis and the group felt ill-equipped to provide help. Of course, they can offer generic encouragement and remind the couple of God's truth. But can you imagine how much richer the experience could have been if the members of the group could confront and comfort with specific understanding of this couple's journey? Better yet, I believe the crisis could have potentially been averted had the couple been transparent in the beginning.

If you don't expose yourself to community, you become isolated while surrounded by people. The enemy wants to get you to that place. The first time you want to keep something to yourself because you don't want to be bothered or you don't want to hear the input of others, the enemy gains ground. When you hold back because you've been hurt before, you choose to protect yourself and minimize the risk of being betrayed, the enemy gains ground. When you're more concerned about embarrassment than the ultimate benefits of exposure, the enemy gains ground.

Exposure is important and a healthy community can make the difference if you're headed down a bad path. Second Samuel 12 is an excellent example of what it looks like when you're open to community. In 2 Samuel 12:1, we see the other side of the familiar story of David. In chapter 11 he messed up – big time. He saw a woman walking on her roof, got said woman pregnant, and killed said woman's husband. Talk about a mess. Chapter 12 opens with "*Then the Lord sent Nathan to David.*" Nathan comes to David and proceeds to tell him a story. This story appears to be about a rich man, poor man, and a lamb. So David is listening attentively and gives his opinion about the selfish actions of the rich man. He even goes so far as to say the rich man deserved death! Nathan knew exactly how to help David see the error of his ways – by helping him to see them in someone else. We're often smart when it comes to assessing others' lives but kind of stupid when it comes to self-assessment. So after David realizes this story is about him, the woman with whom he had an affair, and her husband, he recognized his sin and confessed. He said, "*I have sinned against the LORD.*" In a critical moment of exposure, David confessed to his friend, his community, and opened his heart to the truth and conviction of God. There was punishment for his action but his legacy tells us he was "*a man after His [God's] own heart.*" The reason the Bible can say that David was a man after God's heart is because he opened up his own heart, and even in all of his imperfections he found a way to repent, and he found his way back to the heart of God. We can do that too.

When you're asking God to help you tear down your strongholds, you're asking Him to not only show you what it means to regularly examine your thought life, but what it means to relentlessly expose your thought life to God's Word and to God's people. It won't always be pretty and there are going to be consequences when you've acted based on false truth. You may feel broken at times. But there is beauty in brokenness. Examine it. Expose it.

5.3
ESTABLISH THE TRUTH

Recall earlier in the book when we talked about armies who successfully defeat their enemies. It was due to 1) examination of the target to know how to attack, 2) exposure of the target to the soldiers that will help bring it down, and once the target was defeated, 3) establishment of the new authority. For many of us the new authority, or truth, needs to be *re*-established. We were probably governed by it at one point in our lives but over time we yielded to another authority. We allowed false, convenient, comfortable knowledge to take priority over the absolute, uncomfortable yet freeing knowledge of God.

Truth doesn't merely inform us; it transforms us.

Absolute truth is what tears down strongholds because they thrive on lies. After we expose the lies, they must be uprooted and truth must be established. Truth doesn't merely inform us; it transforms us. One of the reasons I'm passionate about teaching the Bible is because it is literally all you need. Yes, commentaries, lexicons, sermons, etc. can be helpful study tools, but they are resources at best. The Bible is the source. Nothing can replace it. God's Word is the basis of all we believe so if we want to get rid of flawed beliefs, we need be firmly established in truth.

Look at John 8:31-32, "*So Jesus was saying to those Jews who had believed Him, 'If you continue in My word, then you are truly disciples of Mine; and you will know the truth, and the truth shall make you free.'* "

These are extremely important words to internalize as we establish truth. Truth is abiding, or continuing, in the Word of God. It goes beyond the occasional visit that usually happens on the weekends. In verse 31 of this passage, we discover that staying in God's Word will define us as disciples of Jesus. You can hear the truth and not know the truth. Not only does truth change us, and ground us; it defines us. However, these beautiful benefits hinge on knowing the truth, rather than merely hearing it. Yes, this is "knowing" in the biblical sense. We hear it every single Sunday, and some of us even take copious notes and have amazing journals and memos on our devices, but by Tuesday (or Sunday night) you can't remember what truth was given to you. Jesus is telling us we need to be intimate with truth. It's beyond being exposed to truth. This is the result of internalized truth. There's another wonderful benefit to be rooted in truth - freedom. At the end of verse 32, Jesus says, "*And the truth that you know shall set you free.*" Since strongholds are built on bondage of the mind, it's good news that God's truth sets us free.

Freedom does not mean the absence of struggle. Freedom is the absence of slavery.

Freedom does not mean the absence of struggle. Freedom is the absence of slavery. Just because you're no longer a slave, doesn't mean there's no work to be done. Living a free life when we were born slaves can be a daunting challenge. Before Christ, we were slaves to sin, to this world, and to our flesh. Choosing freedom and choosing life require constant counterintuitive thinking and decision-making. We have to fight the flesh every step of the way if we want to walk in freedom. Because even though slavery is horrible, when it becomes familiar, it's easy to drift back into it. It's easy to go back to what's comfortable, what's known, even when it's unhealthy and life-threatening.

A stronghold represents a system of beliefs that has been erected in your life that challenges what's true about God. It's the epicenter of lies. We all have times when we make a wrong decision, but when a stronghold becomes the lens through which we see life, it's time to tear it down and replace the stronghold with the transforming truth of God.

Let's explore a few ways we can establish, or reestablish, truth as our guiding compass.

READ

This is such a simple concept but it's so often neglected. If we want to be established and nourished in truth we need a steady diet of it. Why, you ask? To bring clarity to our feelings. In his book, *Mere Christianity*, C. S. Lewis wrote, "*all your wishes and hopes for the day rush at you like wild animals.*" For most us, just waking up in the morning can be enough to send our minds into overdrive. What will get crossed off the "to-do" list? How will financial obligations be met? What needs to be done at home? What plans need to be made? How will I handle my boss? What's for dinner? (Sometimes that last question is the hardest.) If you mix those, and other questions in with your heart's desires of the day (they are ever-changing), you can see a tornado of thought ready to wreak havoc. Scripture can be bring clarity – and sanity – to the storms in our minds.

We also read to fill up on fresh wisdom. We always need a word from our perfectly wise God. According to Jesus in Matthew 4, we need the Word more than food. I'm going to take a wild guess and say you probably eat every day. Unless you're fasting or extremely busy, you find time to eat something every day. The parallel isn't hard to draw here. If we need God's Word more than food, we *at least* need to take it in daily. Reading the Bible not only answers questions we have, it gives a wealth of knowledge for future questions.

Reading the Bible, improves our fellowship with the Father. Use your reading time to connect with God. What you're reading aren't just words on a page or screen. They are sacred messages from God for our inspiration, information, instruction and more (2 Timothy 3:16-17).

Lastly, reading the Word of God promises prosperity - a prosperity greater than what can be spent. Looking back at Psalm 1, we know that the fruit of freedom and fulfillment only comes when we delight in God's word. You don't have to do a full hour inductive study every day but read *something* from the Bible. It may be a new verse each day – there is a plethora of apps that can give you that. What you read may be one verse or passage that's been on your mind for several days or weeks. It doesn't matter how long the passage is or whether it's Old or New Testament; just read!

Maybe you want to go through a book in the Bible or research various passages on a particular topic. Does approaching the Bible intimidate you? Educate yourself on the structure and messages of the Bible. Learn the beautiful differences between the narratives and poems of the Old Testament in comparison to the epistles (letters) that dominate the New Testament.

Grab a journal or daily devotional that will provide a new passage for you to think about each day. The goal is a steady diet. If you don't read the Bible much right now, set an achievable goal. Don't go from zero to sixty in one day. Once a week may be a significant improvement from where you are today. Do it. Set the goal and go for it. If you fail, just start again. There are no points given for reaching your goal. The goal is for you. It's a path for your growth. Although it's great to use commentaries and other resources, don't get too distracted and miss the heart of the truth you're reading.

REFLECT

Absorb what you read. Take time to ponder and reflect on each truth you take in. Looking again at Psalm 1, the writer encourages us to not simply read God's principles, but meditate on them. Slowing down to think, rather than react, it is imperative in digesting God's truth. Be prepared, this practice is contradictory to the fast pace of most our lives. It may be hard at first but it will yield great reward. Meditation, or reflection, can take various forms based on the individual. If you are a reflective person, you probably do well with just rolling new information over in your mind. Getting somewhere quiet where you just think. If you're easily distracted you may need more concrete reflection methods. For example, I will handwrite a passage of Scripture to reflect on it. (To all the "techies," that actually involves something we call paper and a writing utensil.) I may use my dry erase markers to write an insight or thought on my bathroom mirror, or I may write it on several sticky notes and put them in my various spaces. I create memos on my phone and schedule them like appointments so they pop up randomly throughout my day or week. If you're a visual or creative person, incorporate art and design into your study notes/reminders. The point here is to realize God's Word is life-giving bread and should be savored.

Find ways to reiterate the truth and commit it to memory. You may even want to read the passage in different translations for additional insights.

Discussing what you read with friends or people in your community is another way to help it "stick." The more we talk about something, the more we internalize it. Ask a friend what a particular passage means to them. Start a chat group about it. Another thing I like to do is try to explain a truth I'm reflecting on to our toddler son. It forces me to think simplistically without losing the heart of the message. You can try this on younger children and see how well you communicate God's truth.

If you want to dig deeper, find a book or a study guide (there are several) that walk you through the inductive Bible Study Method. This is a great study method and requires no seminary training. You can start now. Kay Arthur and Howard Hendricks are two of my favorite authors on the topic.

RESPOND

Responding to truth can be the most overlooked aspect of our journey as Christ followers. It's fun to learn more, memorize more, attend more, and know more. I can easily measure those activities. However, responding to the truth that I've read and reflected on can be much more challenging.

In the beginning of this book, I talked about my days as a runner. Sadly, it's a part of my life I had to release after many miles on my knees and other joints. When I was an active runner, I spent a good amount of time managing my diet. I had to intentionally take in enough good calories so I'd have the fuel I needed on my run. If I didn't eat correctly, I would run out of energy and wouldn't be able to finish my run. On the other hand, if I took in the amount of food and calories needed for a run, but never ran, I would still end up tired – and eventually overweight. My intake needed to match my output if I was going to be a successful runner.

This story comes to mind because the Bible says we are runners in this marathon of life. Hebrews 12 (NASB) tells us to "*...run with endurance the race that is set before us, fixing our eyes on Jesus, the author and perfecter of faith,...*" If we are going to run this race well, we need food; it's the runner's fuel. That food is the Word of God; it's fuel and food to our souls. Just like in my example, if we don't take in enough food, we'll be ill-equipped to run the race well. We will stall and stumble and misrepresent our glorious God and become victims of spiritual fatigue. The reverse is also true. If we continue to feast on this amazing food without burning any calories, we will become fat with knowledge. For this reason, it's not enough to read and reflect on truth. In order to be effective, we must respond to truth. It must be seen as essential and necessary to function.

If you want to run the race well, you have to know how to respond in your moment of truth. When you're faced with

If you want to run the race well, you have to know how to respond in your moment of truth.

temptations, desires, shame, fear, or whatever your struggles are, you need to have a response plan. How will you take thoughts captive? How will you tear down the false knowledge against God?

<u>First</u>, you need to invite the Holy Spirit to bring truth to your mind. Jesus promised in John 14:26 (NASB) the Holy Spirit would "*...teach you all things, and bring to your remembrance all that I [Jesus] said to you.*" Try Him. He never fails.

<u>Second</u>, create a script. What do I mean by that? I mean, think about your areas of struggle and create a response for when temptation strikes. You may have noticed that many companies have scripts for their customer service agents and sales representatives to use. These scripts try to ensure a consistent and successful experience for the customer and a sale for the representative. It doesn't matter how great an individual representative is; they need to adhere to the script. The same is true for us. We need to know in advance how to be consistent and successful in responding with truth. If you know you struggle with self-sufficiency and you are presented with a chance to choose independence or community, you need a script. You may use James 4:6 (ESV) to remind yourself that "*God opposes the proud.*" and Galatians 6:2-3 to feel free to share your burden with another. Your script may go something like this "I will choose humility and interdependence in this moment. I will turn away from pride and independence. I will trust God to be my Advocate and give me the strength to share my struggle." Maybe you're faced with an opportunity to lead or step out of your comfortable place and

walk by faith but fear rears its ugly head. You would be wise to remember 1 John 4:18 "*There is no fear in love; but perfect love casts out all fear,...*" and Romans 8:31 "*...If God is for us, who can be against us?*" Your script may read, "God loves me perfectly and there is no room for fear. When I am for Him, He is for me. Faith draws me close to God, but fear creates distance. I cannot move forward unless I choose faith."

I hope you get the idea. It may seem unnecessary or even tedious but giving a voice to the truth that we are reading helps us to respond in the moment. Eventually you won't need to read the words because they'll be internalized. The script is simply applied truth. It's a planned response so you don't become fat from feasting on truth and never putting it to use.

<u>Third</u>, you can find a friend. Not just any friend, of course, but someone from your community. Friends with whom we share our spiritual journey are priceless. I have friends that I can call or text when I'm facing "my moment" and don't trust myself to respond in a way that pleases God. I'm not telling you to develop unhealthy, co-dependent relationships. Ultimately, you must run your own race. But it's a wonderful thing to have others running with you. They can offer truth when you're weak. They can steer you right when wrong looks like a better option. Your community is critical at every stage of destroying strongholds.

Closing Thoughts

Well, you have finally reached the end of this book but it most certainly is not the end of your journey. For many of you, it may only be the beginning. My hope is for you to be stronger after having read this book than you were before you started it. I hope the powerful, life-altering truth of God will permeate every thought, every belief, and every decision. I hope you will commit to staying "armored up," to preventing footholds, and to destroying every fortress and stronghold that exists in your mind. No longer allow the chaos of self-guided truth to reign. Take every thought captive.

I'll leave you with one of my favorite benedictions in Scripture. It's found in 1 Peter 5:6-11. It's packed with instruction and it closes with profound hope.

Humble yourselves, therefore, under the mighty hand of God so that at the proper time He may exalt you, casting all your anxieties on him, because he cares for you. Be sober-minded; be watchful. Your adversary the devil prowls around like a roaring lion, seeking someone to devour. Resist him, firm in your faith, knowing that the same kinds of suffering are being experienced by your brotherhood throughout the world. And after you have suffered a little while, the God of all grace, who has called you to his eternal glory in Christ, will himself restore, confirm, strengthen, and establish you. To him be the dominion forever and ever.

Amen.

Reflection Questions

Ch 1

1. Do you think we can mature as Christ followers by changing our behavior?
2. How important is our thought life (the way we think) to our spiritual growth?
3. Why can our thought life be the most difficult thing to change?
4. What do you think it means to take your "thoughts captive"?

Ch 2

1. Do you believe that Christians are in a spiritual battle? What is the evidence to support your belief?
2. If yes, how have you seen spiritual battles play out in your life? In your family? In your church? In the culture?
3. How attuned are you to the spiritual activity around you? (Scale of 1 to 10)
4. Where are some personal areas of vulnerability?

Ch 3

1. When you think of the enemy (Satan/Devil) what comes to mind?
2. What misconceptions might you have regarding spiritual warfare?
3. How accurate is your idea of the enemy based on what's discussed in this chapter?
4. What piece of armor resonates most strongly with you? (This will change during various seasons of life and faith.)
5. What piece of armor is most difficult for you to put on/keep on?
6. How will you address this area of growth?

Ch 4

1. What is a personal foothold that you're dealing with in this season?
2. If left unaddressed, how could this become a stronghold?
3. Have you seen the Starve/Saturate/Share model work before in your life or in the life of another believer? Which aspect is most challenging for you? (The enemy will discourage you and entice you to take short cuts.)
4. What will you do today to begin addressing the foothold(s) in your life (thinking)?

Ch 5

1. What is a personal stronghold(s) you're facing? How long have you dealt with it?
2. Do you want to tear down this stronghold? (This may seem like an unnecessary question, but it's important that we desire to get well. *See John 5:6.*)
3. When you examine your heart what does God show you?
4. What lies need to be exposed and uprooted in your life?
5. What truth will you plant in place of those uprooted lies? (It's important to have a "cheat sheet" of truth. What Scriptures, promises, principles from God do you need to keep written down or memorize?)

Acknowledgements

Joah - thank you for making me a mother. One day, when you can read this, you'll read that I'm forever grateful that God picked me and your daddy to be your parents. You are a gift and you teach me about joy every day. You are an answer to prayer.

Clyde and Barbara Edwards – thank you for loving me as your daughter. You gave me Conway then you gave me you. Mom Edwards you are kind, gracious, sincere, and the epitome of a servant. Dad Edwards, I could sit at your feet and listen to your wisdom for days. You have given me, and Conway, the high standard of faithfulness in ministry and marriage to strive for. I love you.

Dr. Tony and Lois Evans – thank you for your love and example. You have set the standard for grace, truth, perseverance, and excellence in ministry. You have loved me like a daughter and my husband like a son. We are a part of your legacy.

Rhoda Gonzales – my mentor and friend. Your unfiltered truth has shaped me significantly. Your prayer life should be the aim of every believer. The Lord was gracious when he brought you into my life and I'm grateful for you.

My Tribe – thank you for being inspirational women. You are my iron and you sharpen me. You are my village of sanity, comedy, and secrets. (shhh. You have made independence an impossibility. I need you. To Tresa (sissy!, Cheri, Talisha, Shanterra, Nicole, Chrystal, Michelle, Priscilla, and Shundria – I love you beyond these words.

Priscilla Shirer – thank you friend for giving guidance in this process. You are a trailblazer and I'm proud to have you in my tribe. You have set a high standard for serving women and it's my joy to witness your journey.

One Community Church – thank you for eight great years. Thanks to the Creative Ministry that has given me the privilege of leading them for the past eight years. Thanks to the Women's team and all the women of One that hang out with me on Wednesdays while we explore God's word together. Thank you to the dedicated staff that works tirelessly for our vision and for the Kingdom. Sue, Renee, and Cathy, thanks for editing. Marlon, this cover is amazing. Andrea, you were critical to this final product. Much love to our amazing volunteers who keep us running smoothly. My heart is for you One Community.